Terrorism

Also available from Continuum:

Think Now

Think Now is a brand new series of stimulating and accessible books examining key contemporary social issues from a philosophical perspective. Written by experts in philosophy, these books offer sophisticated and provocative yet engaging writing on political and cultural themes of genuine concern to the educated reader.

The Ethics of Climate Change, James Garvey

Identity Crisis, Jeremy Stangroom

War and Ethics, Nicholas Fotion

Terrorism, Nicholas Fotion, Boris Kashnikov and Joanne K. Lekea

Series Editors:

James Garvey is Secretary of The Royal Institute of Philosophy and author of *The Twenty Greatest Philosophy Books* (Continuum).

Jeremy Stangroom is co-editor, with Julian Baggini, of *The Philosophers' Magazine* and co-author of *Why Truth Matters*, *What Philosophers Think* and *Great Thinkers A–Z* (all Continuum).

Terrorism

The New World Disorder

Nicholas Fotion, Boris Kashnikov and
Joanne K. Lekea

continuum

Continuum
The Tower Building
11 York Road
London SE1 7NX

80 Maiden Lane
Suite 704
New York
NY 10038

www.continuumbooks.com

British Library Cataloguing-in-Publication Data
A catalogue record for this book is available from the British Library.

ISBN: HB: 0-8264-9257-6
      9780826492579

      PB: 0-8264-9258-4
      9780826492586

Library of Congress Cataloging-in-Publication Data
A catalog record for this book is available from the Library of Congress.

Typeset by BookEns Ltd, Royston, Herts.
Printed and bound in Great Britain by MPG Books, Bodmin, Cornwall.

Contents

Abbreviations and Glossary

Al-Aqsa (Martyrs) Brigade	Radical Palestinian wing of Fatah. Suicide terrorism is their speciality.
Al-Fatah	(Victory) Palestinian resistance group founded by Yasser Arafat in 1956. Al Fatah, under Arafat, gained control of the PLO by the late 1960s.
Al-Qaeda	Islamic terrorist group founded in 1988 by Osama Bin Laden. Its chief target is the United States.
Assassins	Medieval Islamic suicide terrorists.
Black September	Militant wing of the PLO. Black September is most famous for its attack on the Olympic Village in Munich (1972). The organization was disbanded in the mid-1970s.
Black Tigers	Radical terrorist group formed within LTTE.
Black Widows	Chechen female suicide terrorists. Most, but not all, of the Black Widows had lost their husbands in the fighting with the Russians.
caliphate	Islamic government ruled by a caliph (or successor) to Muhammad.

discrimination principle	A principle in the *jus in bello* portion of just war theory that separates those who can be targeted in war (e.g. armed enemy soldiers) from those who should not be targeted (e.g. children).
ELA	(Revolutionary Popular Fight) A left-wing Greek terrorist group formed in 1974, the ELA specialized in targeting buildings.
fedayeen	Literally, one who sacrifices himself. An Islamic warrior.
GAM	(Gerakin Aceh Markeda) Free Aceh Movement.
Hamas	Islamic resistance movement. A Sunni Islamic fundamentalist movement operating primarily in and around Gaza. Now controls Palestinian government.
Hezbollah	The Party of God. Shiite Islamic fundamentalist movement originating in Lebanon. It is supported by Syria but more especially by Iran.
intifada	(Lit. 'shaking off'.) Palestinian uprisings against Israel. The first took place between 1987 and 1990; the second between 2000 and 2004.
IPKF	Indian peace-keeping force serving in Sri Lanka to quell the troubles between the Tamils and the Sinhala.
IRA	(Irish Republican Army) Founded in 1919, the IRA fought first for an independent Irish state, and later for the unification of Northern Ireland and the Irish Free State (Eire) into one independent Irish republic.

Irgun (Irgun Zvai Leumi)	Jewish terrorist group active in Palestine during the British mandate years.
Islamic Jihad	A collection of loosely affiliated terrorist groups from Egypt and Palestine. Islamic Jihad targets corrupt Islamic political leaders as well as Western governments and their populations.
Janjaweed	Nomadic group of tribes in Sudan. The Janjaweed militia are responsible for much of the killing of black Africans in western Sudan (Darfur).
jihad	Struggle in the way of God (Allah). The struggle can be one of conscience against Satan or it can be a war against non-believers (especially those who threaten Islam).
jus ad bellum	(Justice of the war) Part of just war theory concerning when a nation has a moral right to go to war.
jus in bello	Justice in the war. Part of just war theory having to do with the prosecution of a just war.
just cause principle	Principle of the *jus ad bellum* aspect of just war theory. Also called the good reasons' principle. Its most prominent feature is to allow a nation or group to enter a war if it or an ally is responding to aggression. The principle also allows entry into war in order to stop a humanitarian catastrophe.
Kamikaze	Term used to describe Japanese pilots who flew suicide bombing missions during the Second World War.

last resort principle	A principle from the *jus ad bellum* strand of just war theory that counsels caution when there is a temptation to go to war. It advises that a series of steps be taken before war is declared.
LTTE	(Liberation Tigers of Tamil Eelan) Hindu rebel group from Sri Lanka opposed to dominant Buddhist group (Sinhalese people).
Mossad	Israeli secret service.
17 November	Revolutionary Organization 17 November. Greek terrorist group formed in 1975 to target corrupt government officials. In its terrorist activities it was careful not to harm the people of Greece that it claimed it was fighting for.
People's Will	Late nineteenth-century Russian terrorist organization.
PIRA	Provisional Irish Republican Army (Provos). The PIRA split from the official IRA in 1969.
PKK	(Partia Karkaren Kurdistan) Terrorist organization in Turkey fighting for the independence of the Kurdish people.
PLO	(Palestine Liberation Organization) Originally founded in 1964 by the Arab states to create a democratic Palestinian state to supplement the State of Israel. Later, under Yasser Arafat, the PLO modified its aim to that of establishing an independent Palestinian state alongside that of Israel.
PS	Paradigmatic Scheme of just war theory.
RAF	Royal Air Force (British).

'Q' ships   Heavily armed, but disguised, merchant ships in the First World War.

Shiites   Followers of Ali (cousin of Muhammad). Shiites believe that the line of successors (caliphs) should be inherited.

SLA   (Sudan Liberation Army) One rebel group, among others, fighting the Sudanese government and the janjaweed for the liberation of the 'black' peoples in the Darfur region of Sudan.

SR   Socialist Revolutionary Party operating in Russia during the early years of the twentieth century.

Stern Gang (Lehi)   Jewish terrorist group founded during the Second World War. Its purpose was to drive both the British and Arab people from Palestine.

Sunni   The majority line of Islam through the history of the religion. Sunnis believe that the successors (caliphs) to Muhammad should not be inherited but rather should be chosen by a consensus of the group's leaders.

Taliban   Students of Islamic knowledge. Fundamentalist Islamic party that ruled most of Afghanistan between 1996 and 2001.

Tamil Tigers   See LTTE.

umma   World community of Muslims.

Preface

This is a work on the *ethics* of terrorism. One of its aims is to assess how ethical or unethical terrorism is. So the questions we answer in this work include the following. Is practising terrorism automatically immoral (unethical)? If not, under what conditions is terrorism not immoral? Is terrorism any worse ethically (morally) than other forms of killing in war and/or war-like settings?

A second aim is to assess the ethics or morality of the response to terrorism. We deal with the following questions: Is it proper to respond to terrorism with terrorism? Are the principles that guide nations and groups in responding to terrorism the same as those when they respond during war to traditional enemy states?

Taken together, these two aims mean that this study must look at terrorism not just from the point of view of its victims. Precious little understanding of the ethics of terrorism accrues by simply looking at terrorism from that point of view. But we have two other aims in this work. We aim to look at both major forms of terrorism. The first is sometimes called martyr terrorism. It is also called suicide terrorism. For the lack of a better term, we call the second kind escape terrorism. With the former, those who perform a terrorist act pay a price. One member of the terrorist group gives up his or her life. With the latter the terrorists do what they do, but somehow escape from the scene of their 'crime'. Our aim is to look at both kinds of terrorism, but to give special attention to martyr terrorism. There are three reasons for giving this form of terrorism such attention. First, it apparently has the greatest growth potential. Increasingly, it appears to be the chosen means of both sectarian and secular terrorists. Second, as a relatively new form of terrorism, it is less understood. It thus behoves anyone who discusses the ethics of terrorism to examine this form more carefully before making ethical judgements about terrorism as a whole. Third, it can be argued that martyr terrorism is important if for no other reason than it appears to be so extremely effective.

But escape terrorism is also important in its own right, and so needs to be studied as well. This needs to be done for another reason. It is helpful in understanding the special interest we have in martyr terrorism to contrast that form with escape terrorism. In that connection, we will answer the following questions: Is martyr terrorism really more dangerous than any form of escape terrorism? Does one or the other form require more training, patience and perpetrators than the other?

In this book, we first describe terrorism and then assess it. The first two chapters consider the theory of terrorism. In Chapter 1 we ask the following questions: Is there any agreement as to how terrorism is defined? Can it be defined even if there is no general agreement about the definition? Are there various forms of terrorism? Who are the victims of terrorism? Must these victims always be 'innocents' in war? Is it always easy to tell when a terrorist act is taking place? Is a terrorist act still a terrorist act if it fails to terrorize?

Chapter 2 examines martyr terrorism and asks: What is martyr terrorism? How does it differ from other forms of martyrdom? How does it differ from other forms of terrorism? Are there several forms of martyr terrorism? Are martyr terrorists mostly sectarian? Is martyr terrorism a new phenomenon?

In Chapters 3 and 4 we present case-studies of terrorism. Chapter 3 begins with a discussion of Russian revolutionary terrorism and goes on to look at terrorism during the two World Wars and beyond, in Northern Ireland, Greece and elsewhere. So also are cases from the First and Second World Wars: namely., the blockades of the First

World War and the British bombings of Germany in the Second World War. The Japanese kamikazes are also discussed in this chapter. So also are cases from Ireland, Aceh on the island of Sumatra, and Greece. Two kinds of cases, and some in between, will be found in this and the next chapter. There are classic cases, so called because almost everyone recognizes them as terrorism. These cases satisfy all of the criteria of terrorism identified in Chapter 1. The second kind is made up of marginal cases. These don't satisfy all of the criteria but they satisfy many. Featuring these cases takes the analysis of the concept of terrorism to the limit. These cases, then, force us to think seriously about the border between those acts and campaigns that fall on one or the other side of the terrorism border.

Chapter 4 discusses recent and ongoing cases of terrorism, including the conflicts in Sri Lanka, Chechnya, Darfur, Israel/Lebanon/Palestine, and Iraq. We also look at al-Qaeda in this chapter.

The final chapters deal with general considerations regarding terrorism. Chapter 5 explores the political and military causes of terrorism, and deals with the following questions: Is state terrorism significantly different from non-state terrorism? Is the motivation of state terrorism different from that of non-state terrorism? Do non-state terrorist movements thrive if the nation their members work in has a corrupt government? Do these movements thrive when their nation is being occupied by some foreign power? What if that foreign power has a different religion from the nation being occupied? Does martyr terrorism occur (mainly, exclusively?) because a nation is being occupied?

Chapter 6 examines the personal reasons that lead people to become terrorists. Are terrorists loners or do they, on most occasions, act under the guidance of special people from their social group? Are martyr terrorists significantly different from escape terrorists?

Chapter 7 considers the outlook for terrorism, including such issues as recruitment, funding and organization. Is terrorism likely to continue? If it is, is it because there are always 'causes' for which they choose to fight? Is it because it is relatively easy to recruit new members? To fund terrorism? To organize terrorist groups? Is it because there are so many targets for terrorists to kill, maim and/or destroy? All the above?

Chapter 8 explores the justification of terrorism. Are terrorists completely and without question immoral? Or, in spite of what they do, can they be viewed as operating within the moral realm? Do they view themselves as acting morally? If they do, do terrorists present arguments that show that they are morally justified in acting as they do? How many different arguments do they have? Do most of their arguments rest on their claim that the people whom terrorists represent are victims of oppression and exploitation? What of the claim, often articulated by many terrorists, that if they really can be called terrorists, they are terrorists on a small scale. On a big scale, so their claim goes, the terrorists are the major states such as the United States, Great Britain, and Russia.

Chapter 9 offers some criticisms of terrorism in the light of just war theory. Does terrorism violate all the considerations of the just war, or only some of them? What about *jus in bello* (justice concerned with how wars are fought)? Do terrorists violate all or none of these principles? In short, is terrorism completely immoral? Or is it to be criticized for violating some of that theory's principles? If only some, which principles do terrorists violate?

Finally in Chapter 10, we look at what can be done about terrorism and place our recommendations under three headings. The first deals with military responses to terrorism. Given that terrorism can sprout almost anywhere and at any time, how can war on terrorism ever be won? Is it important to fight terrorism by holding onto the 'high moral ground'? Or is it better (or smarter) to fight dirt with dirt? Terrorism with terrorism? The second heading concerns international (external), non-military steps for its containment. Here are some of the questions under that heading. Is diplomacy useful in containing terrorism or is it, largely, a waste of time? How important is it, if it is important at all, for nations to cooperate with one another in dealing with terrorism? The discussion under the third heading focuses on what internal steps a nation can take to control terrorism. Can a blanket of security cover a nation so that it can be made immune from terrorist attacks? Does it make sense to educate one's people so that they do not overreact to terrorism? Is there any connection between a nation's energy-use policies and terrorism?

1 Terrorism

On defining terrorism

Discussions of terrorism traditionally start with a search for a definition. The motive behind this search is as old as philosophy. We are told that you cannot discuss any subject until you make it clear what it is you are talking about. So to discuss terrorism intelligently, a definition of that concept must be presented up front. But immediately, we face a problem somewhat special to the concept of terrorism. Walter Laqueur reports that there are more than a hundred definitions in the literature.[1] How is one to choose among them? Or should one invent yet another definition so as to add to the list?

One reason terrorism is so difficult to define is that it is often interpreted as a pejorative concept.[2] Whatever the final meaning of the term turns out to be, those who are identified as terrorists are said to be deserving of blame. It is somewhat akin to calling someone a thief, a liar, a rapist or a murderer. As a result, those who are regularly accused of being terrorists are keen to look for a definition that will not apply to them. 'What we do in killing people in shopping centres is not terrorism', they might say, 'it is part of our effort to liberate our people. Rather than being terrorists we are freedom-fighters.' In contrast, their accusers are all too anxious to define terrorism in such a way that this nasty term sticks to their enemies.

Another reason why it is difficult to define 'terrorism', 'terrorist', etc. is that these terms are used in highly emotive settings. We have a pre-definitional sense that they are associated with death, violence and war. In such emotional settings we tend to become linguistically complacent, and so tend to let our language develop fuzzy edges. Thus, after a while, the terminology we associate with terrorism becomes so vague that almost any enemy action comes to have the label of terrorism attached to it.

It is not surprising, therefore, that philosophers, political theorists and others who are concerned to understand these terms develop a strong urge to rein in their meanings. They despair of finding the meaning of each of these terms in how they are used in our natural language.[3] Our natural language is said to be too confused, having developed over time from different traditions, to give us a clear and consistent portrait of such a complicated concept as terrorism. So they say that they need to add their own definition to the already long list of proposed definitions.

To be sure, the different definitions these thinkers offer us tell us different things. Some tell us that terrorism is mainly an activity of the state, others that it is mainly an activity of non-state groups, and still others that it encompasses both states and non-state groups. Other definitions focus on the victims of terrorism. They tell us that if an act is terrorist in nature only if 'innocents' (i.e. civilians, non-participants in a war, etc.) are the victims.[4] Still others say that the victims can be 'innocents' *and* non-innocents. Finally, others focus on one or more of the emotions that terrorism engenders, and also on the effects of these emotions. Concerning the effects, some tell us that they must be political only while others say they need not be.

In this study we will *not* attempt to take on what is probably the hopeless task of finding the true, correct, best, etc. definition of terrorism. Instead, we will propose a rough characterization of terrorism and the family of terms that surround it. Instead of presenting a strict definition that shows cleanly and clearly what the borders of these terms are, we will be content to present a characterization where the borders are left somewhat fuzzy. In addition to being fuzzy, the borders will be broad. With narrow definitions and characterizations, there is a danger of arbitrarily leaving certain things out of the discussion that deserve attention. Our broader characterization does not suffer from that fault. Further, because of its broadness it can, when necessary, take in ideas that the narrow view of terrorism are prone to express. As it will become evident, our rough and broad characterization is all that is needed to discuss the various forms of terrorism.

A rough characterization

Terrorism can be viewed as a tactic in a war or in some sort of war-like struggle. It is a tactic for getting one's way that can be used by nations, non-nation groups and even individuals. No doubt there are many ways of 'getting one's way'. At one extreme, reasoning with one's opponent might be tried. Failing that, propaganda might be tried. And failing even that, social and political pressure might be applied. If all these moves fail, some form of violence might seem the only option left. On the individual level, the violence might take the form of beatings or killings. On the larger social scene, the violence might turn to war.

But going to war is more a strategic move that groups make rather than a tactical one. Tactics come into play when those who are in charge of the war decide how it is to be conducted. When appropriate, the tactics might involve blockade, siege warfare, frontal assaults, bombardment, envelopment, and so on. But, when appropriate, terrorism might be instead the tactic of choice.[5]

Looking at terrorism as a tactic in war and war-like struggles leaves open the possibility that anyone can employ terrorism against anyone. State forces can employ terrorism against: (a) state forces from another state; (b) groups, people and/or officials of another state; (c) some of the people and officials of their own state; or (d) non-state forces from their own state. On the other side, non-state forces can employ terrorism against: (a) other non-state forces in their own land; (b) some (or all) of the people in their own land; (c) some (or all) of the people in another land; or (d) state forces in their own or another land. Not only do terrorists have *carte blanche* with respect to targets, they have, if not *carte blanche*, a wide variety of options as to how they might strike their enemy.

Listed below are the rough characterizations of terrorism, and more particularly, of a terrorist act. What is labelled the paradigmatic scheme represents the most generally accepted form of such an act. The variations of the scheme help show how complicated the concept of terrorism is.

Paradigmatic scheme (PS) An attacking group (or individual) victimizes some group of people by harming or killing them. The attackers then escape either before, during or after the victimizing event. Others, seeing what has happened to the victim group become terrorized (frightened, anxious, etc.). We will call this the immediate effect or result of the process of creating victims. While in their state of terror, they pressure their government to change its political outlook in a way that satisfies the goals of the attackers and, most likely, displeases the government and many of its people. This pressure and resulting changes count as the secondary effect or result of the victimization process.

Variation 1 of PS All is the same as with PS, except the secondary result is not a change of outlook of the victim government but a weakening of that government. This variation of PS can come about because the frightened people realize that their government can no longer protect them. So they lose confidence in it and, perhaps, abandon it in favour of the attackers and/or their sympathizers.

Variation 2 of PS All is the same except that the secondary result is that those who are terrorized change their behaviour (e.g. by leaving the country that the attackers want to be ethnically cleansed –

fleeing into the mountains, woods or jungle, and quitting their jobs).

Variation 3 of PS Instead of harming or killing a victim group, the attackers threaten a target group. The threatened group and the larger (enemy) population are terrorized into behaving in accordance with PS, or Variation 1 or 2.

Variation 4 of PS The attackers operate under the flag of PS, or Variation 1 or 2, but do not escape. Instead they become martyrs.

Problem

The above rough characterization of terrorism is indeed broad in scope and so stands in sharp contrast with various narrower characterizations and definitions of that concept. Typically, supporters of the narrower view insist that the victims of terrorism must be 'innocent' (i.e. be non-participants in the war, civilians, etc.). On these accounts, attacks on police, military personnel, key government officials, even if these people are terrorized, are not really acts of terrorism. Instead, they fall under such headings as guerrilla warfare or assassination.

This narrower sense of terrorism has some advantages over the broader sense that we are using. In the first place, it focuses attention on the fact that the vast majority of acts that could be described as terrorist are aimed at 'innocents'. Secondly, it is much easier on this account to identify alleged acts of terrorism as real acts of terrorism. The narrower meaning is less vague.

In contrast, the broad sense of terrorism involves identification problems. Because it allows for the possibility that terrorism can target non-innocents, it must deal with the following kinds of question. Is this attack on a police station an act of terrorism or is it part of an ongoing guerrilla war? Is that attack on some military recruits an act of terrorism or is it also part of the guerrilla war? Is this killing of the minister of transportation terrorism or is it assassination?

In answering these questions notice, first of all, that there is no law of logic that requires ease in identifying cases of such a complex phenomenon as terrorism. Of course identifying cases of terrorism can be made easy by definition. That result is achieved by those who offer us the narrow meaning of terrorism. But remember their definitions are narrow because they have chosen to make them so. Their choice, no doubt, is guided largely by the already observed fact that most alleged acts of terrorism are aimed at innocents. But their choice to <u>narrow the definition of terrorism</u> also faces a problem. There are certain violent attacks on, for example, non-innocent police personnel that look and sound like acts of terrorism. To see this, imagine that Police Station 2 has been attacked and all the police stationed there are either killed or later executed. Let us further imagine that the morale among the police in the region is already pretty low. Once the news of what happened at Station 2 comes to be generally known, police at Stations 1, 3 and 4 nearby abandon their posts. They <u>are too frightened to go back to work</u>. We can further imagine that whatever happened was in accordance with the attackers' plan. What has happened in Police Station 2 sounds very much as if it fits Variation 2 of PS.

We can imagine a similar scenario (as happened in Iraq) where the victims are raw recruits in the military. They too, once some of their kind have been victimized, flee the military camp and become civilians once more. A few of those who have fled later join one of the terrorist groups.

It is clear that these attacks on the police and the soldiers have all the hallmarks of attacks that everyone would identify as terrorist in nature (see Variation 2). The only feature they lack is that these attacks are not aimed at innocents. But that is the feature under dispute in identifying a characterization or definition of terrorism. So it can hardly be cited as a reason for favouring the narrow version without begging the question.

Further, the characterization of terrorism offered here does not need to deny that innocents are most often the victims of terrorism.

All it needs to deny is that innocence is a part of the meaning of terrorism. That is, it denies that innocence is a necessary condition for an act or campaign to be labelled terrorist. According to our characterization, then, it is possible to perform acts of terrorism on innocents and/or on non-innocents. Indeed, we can easily imagine attackers targeting 'innocents' one day, raw recruits the next day, more innocents on another day and police stations on yet another day. It is not as if these attackers are concerned to make fine distinctions between being terrorists in attacking 'innocents' one day, and then being something else when they attack those who are not innocent. In their eyes, they are doing the same kind of work no matter whom they attack. No matter whom they attack, they seem to be in the terrorism business.

The broad account of terrorism we are presenting gains plausibility if certain distinctions are made. One such distinction is between terrorism and guerrilla war. It might be thought that a series of attacks must count as either terrorism or part of a guerrilla war. On this account, if the attack is on innocents then, most likely, it is terrorist; if it is an ambush of military or police personnel, then it is a guerrilla attack. It is one or the other, but it cannot be both. But such dichotomous thinking is misguided. Ambushes can be executed simply by way of killing enemy personnel, and thereby weakening their forces. But they can also be executed in order to terrorize the enemy into abandoning their posts. Combinations are possible as well. Ambushes can both destroy the enemy's military potential and terrorize. Put differently, guerrillas are still guerrillas when they employ the tactic of terrorism and when they do not. But they can also be called terrorists if, indeed, they employ the tactic of terrorism on a regular basis. It is not as if when you are a terrorist you cannot also be a guerrilla fighter.

The same point applies when nations engage in terrorism. During the Second World War, the RAF's Bomber Command regularly employed terrorist tactics in their attacks on German cities (see case-study in Chapter 3). But the airmen who did this terrorist bombing were, nonetheless, still counted as military personnel who also engaged in conventional warfare. It wasn't as if when they bombed cities they had shed their regular military status and become terrorists pure and simple; and when they bombed German military targets they were no longer terrorists, but just regular RAF guys.

The same point can be made when discussing assassinations. It might be tempting to argue that killing a high official of a government is an assassination and so cannot be an act of terrorism. It might be just that: an assassination. But, if the circumstances are right, an assassination can also be an act of terrorism. The two concepts are not necessarily opposed to one another so that if someone is an assassin he cannot be a terrorist, and if he is a terrorist he cannot be, strictly speaking, an assassin.

The upshot of these analyses is that none of these distinctions can be used to distinguish terrorism from non-terrorism in a clear and sharp way. There are acts of violence that are clearly terrorist in nature and nothing else. Other acts have nothing to do with terrorism (e.g. as when tanks roll over defences and smash the opposition). But there are still other acts that create a blur between terrorism and non-terrorism. An example here would be a well-publicized attack on enemy troops that both kills many of them (and so weakens the enemy army) *and* sends a message to others that the same fate awaits them if they continue to resist. Cases like these will make it difficult to describe what is happening. Different reporters of the event will describe it differently. Some will use the terrorist concepts in this setting, others will not. This blurring between terrorism and many of the other concepts of violence is unavoidable.

But there is another reason why these concepts are difficult to apply. An imaginary story helps to show why. A police station blows up in a south-east Asian country killing one officer and wounding others. Bomb materials are found, so it is clear that the explosion was not an accident. Even so, no one panics. No one is terrorized. And no one claims (dis)credit for the bombing.

Change the situation slightly. Everything is the same except that a home of a government official is destroyed, and one family member is killed and others injured. Change it once more. Now the home of an ordinary citizen blows up with one death and some injuries. Are these acts of terrorism or not? The fact that no one is terrorized does not prove that these are not terrorist acts. It could be that the victims are enraged rather than terrorized, or that they are so accustomed to violence that their response to it is cool indifference.

It certainly would help if the attackers said something publicly about their intentions. But suppose they keep their silence perhaps because they too ashamed to admit their failure as terrorists. So those involved in trying to understand why these bombings took place are left wondering whether the bombings were acts of revenge, random violence of an insane or drug-crazed person, terrorist acts, or some combination.

One might ask at this point what else could those who are trying to understand these bombings do? Actually, they could do several things, but none is easy. They could systematically eliminate other explanations for the bombings. They could explore whether anyone was seeking revenge against the police, the government official or the ordinary citizen. Or they could compare these bombings with other recent bombings that actually did terrorize. Or, if that option yielded no results, they could wait to see if future bombings resembled the bombings described above. But, in truth, all these efforts might fail. That is the point. Given the nature of terrorism, it often isn't clear who committed the terrorist act, why it was committed and, at times, it is not even clear that the act was one of terrorism in the first place.

Summary so far

We can summarize the characteristics of terrorism as follows:

1. The paradigmatic scheme (PS) identifies three groups of people who are at the receiving end of terrorism. There are the victims, those who are terrorized and those who respond to the pressures

from the terrorized. Also, there are variations on PS that show that terrorism is not an easy-to-understand phenomenon.

2. A plausible case can be made for the broad characterization of terrorism (and its related concepts). Viewed as a tactic used in situations of violent conflict, there seems to be no principled way to distinguish between attacks on 'innocents' and on those who are not innocent such that the former can be called terrorist attacks and the latter something else.

3. Some attacks will be difficult to classify as terrorist in nature. This is because these attacks are a mixture of conventional warfare and terrorism. This difficulty does not so much represent a weakness in our broad characterization of terrorism as it does reality. War and war-like conflict involve the use of many different kinds of tactics either singly or in combination. It should be no surprise, therefore, that the tactic of terrorism is used at times in tandem with other military tactics.

4. Just as it is not always easy to identify attacks as acts of terrorism, it is similarly not easy to identify attackers as terrorists. In fact, some will be easy to characterize as terrorists. If all their attacks follow PS or one or more of its variants, they are terrorists pure and simple. They are terrorists as well if they engage in a single attack, say, on a shopping centre or a railway station full of ordinary citizens. It becomes more difficult to classify perpetrators as terrorists when their attacks are a mixture of regular military actions (e.g. where valuable military equipment is destroyed and military personnel are killed) and terrorism (e.g. where in addition to the destruction they cause, the attackers have a clear intent to frighten their opponents into abandoning their posts).

Ethical implications

Since this is a work primarily in the realm of ethics, it is important for us to make clear what ethical implications our broad conception of terrorism carries with it. These implications can only be fully understood toward the end of this work rather than at the beginning. Still, certain things need to be said in order to get the process of understanding started.

As we have already noted, terrorism is a pejorative concept for many who concern themselves with issues having to do with its ethics. Primarily this is so because terrorists kill innocents on a regular basis, and such killing is condemned by almost all general moral theories. So it is needlessly duplicative to show why each of these theories abhors the killing of innocents. All that is needed is to show that what is universally called just war theory condemns such killing. The reason appealing to just war theory is enough is that as a less general theory, it is widely accepted by theorists who defend the more general (major) ethical theories. Typically, these theories carry such labels as contractualism, utilitarianism and Kantianism. Since all these theories can be used to derive versions of just war theory, this makes that theory a kind of coin of the realm.

Here, briefly, is what just war theory tells us about war and war-like situations. (A fuller version of this theory will be developed in later chapters.) The theory divides ethical issues in war into two parts.[6] The first deals with the start of war and war-like activities. That part tells us that any nation or group intent on starting a war must meet a series of conditions or tests. Traditionally, although it varies from time to time and theorist to theorist, there are six conditions to be met. Beyond that, the theory tells us explicitly that each and every condition (or test) must be met. Otherwise, the war one engages in is said to be unjust, wrong, immoral, etc. The second part of the theory deals with moral issues that arise once the war starts. There are two principles in this part of the theory.

Here are the six conditions or principles for the first part of the theory, with a brief explanation of each.

Part 1 Justice of the war (*jus ad bellum*)

1. *Just cause* This condition tells us that a nation or group enters into war or war-like activity justly only if it has at least one good reason for doing so. Typical good reasons are that one's nation or group is already under attack or has recently been attacked; one's ally is under attack or has recently been attacked; one is about to be attacked (i.e. the attack is imminent and serious); or that a people need to be saved from some form of humanitarian disaster. Excluded from the list of good reasons is going to war to promulgate one's ideology (e.g. Christianity, communism, fascism, democracy). Also excluded are such reasons as expanding a nation's borders and gaining important resources (e.g. uranium, gold). In sum, a nation meets the just cause test only if it is responding to some form of aggression or catastrophe. *– self-defense only.*

Note?

2. *Right intentions* A nation or group has right intentions in entering a conflict when its behaviour is guided largely by the good reasons for which they went to war. Thus a nation has good intentions if it enters a war in order to undo the aggression it faces, but it does not have good intentions if it uses the war to gain land and resources that do not belong to it. It should not be assumed that a nation's good intentions must be pure. So long as the good reason contributes significantly to guiding the nation's behaviour it is acceptable that it also has some self-interest intentions that influence the decision to go to war. If purity were the test, no nation could ever satisfy the good intentions principle. It is impossible to imagine a government, made up of various powerful officials with differing views and attitudes, all agreeing that the only guiding reason for going to war is, for example, to stop a humanitarian catastrophe.

3. *Proportionality* According to this condition, going to war is just if it can be predicted that more good than evil will come from a war. Conversely, if it can be predicted that millions of people will die in order to save a few thousand lives, then the war is unjust. But

eg

because many wars are so unpredictable, the importance of this principle for just war theory can be questioned.

4. *Likelihood of success* Starting a war with a small military force that is facing a modern and powerful military machine is unjust. One must have some reasonable prospect of achieving a military or political end before a nation or a group can justly go to war. As with the proportionality principle, the uncertainty of war limits the application of this principle.

5. *Last resort* No nation or group should go to war before it has tried to avoid war by resorting to other means (e.g. negotiations, sanctions). The term 'last' in this principle should not be taken too seriously, since no resort identifies itself as the last one before the start of war. Rather, what this important principle conveys is that a long series of steps should be taken before visiting the horrors of war on an enemy and one's own nation. The principle does not tell us how long the series should be. Presumably in some situations (e.g. when nations face the prospect of another world war) the series should be extremely long. Nations should not allow themselves to stumble into a war as in the case of the First World War.

6. *Legitimate authority* War must be entered into only by those who are authorized to embark upon it. Certain leaders in each society have the power to start a war. We might say they have a monopoly when it comes to starting a war. Should others – for example, a group of private citizens – actually precipitate a war in which many people die, that war would be unjust. Since the Second World War, this principle has become more difficult to apply because of the United Nations. Some claim that when nations or groups of nations engage in a war for humanitarian purposes, only the UN is the legitimate authority. Others say that nations still hold the final say concerning the legitimacy of all wars.

Part 2 Justice in the war (*jus in bello*)

1. *Proportionality* Like proportionality in part 1 of just war theory, proportionality *jus in bello* tells us that our actions should be expected to do more good than harm. But in part 2, the balance of good to harm is concerned with battles and campaigns rather than with the war as a whole.

2. *Discrimination* This principle tells us that certain people, animals and facilities should not be attacked, while others can be. Those not to be attacked include children, the elderly, mothers-to-be, secretaries working in civilian businesses, doctors, religious leaders and prisoners. Facilities that are immune from attack include hospitals, schools, civilian airliners and religious institutions. Those who can be attacked include armed and uniformed soldiers and sailors, munitions workers and those transportation workers who serve the military. Objects that can be attacked include tanks, armoured personnel carriers, military aircraft, naval ships and trains supplying the military. Facilities that can be attacked include military camps and airfields, naval dockyards and munitions factories. What can and cannot be attacked varies with the situation on the battlefield. For example, if a war is almost over, even munitions factories might become immune from attack, since the shells they produce will never reach the front-line in time to be used in battle. On the other hand, a school that would normally be immune might be attacked if the enemy has set up snipers in it.

We will eventually see that, as described, just war theory needs to be modified in order to deal with certain forms of terrorism. The main reason for this is that historically just war theory has been viewed as a theory to help deal with wars between nation-states. But many terrorist wars or conflicts are between a nation, on the one side, and a non-nation rebel group, on the other. However, even though it will need to be modified, the traditional version of just war theory can still be useful at the beginning of this work since it does in fact share much with the modified version of the theory that we will eventually develop and employ.

Before doing that, it is important to discuss terrorism itself in more depth. We will do that in the chapters that follow, some of which focus on certain important variations, especially on martyr (or suicide) terrorism.

As explained, our rough version of terrorism is broad in scope and so contrasts with various narrower versions. In what follows, we will work mainly with the broad version to see how it helps us in understanding and making a moral assessment of terrorism. However, for the sake of those who prefer one of the narrower versions, we will also work with some of these versions as well. There is nothing illogical about gaining an understanding and making a moral assessment of terrorism along two or more lines in tandem. Indeed, as we will see, there is an advantage in doing so.

One of the narrower versions is exactly like the broad version, except that it specifies that the victims of terrorism are 'innocents' (non-combatants, those not involved directly in the war effort, etc.). Here are the schemes for this version.

Narrow paradigmatic scheme (NPS) An attacking group victimizes a group of 'innocents' by harming or killing them and, either before, during or after the victimizing event, escapes. Other innocents, seeing what has happened to the victim group, become terrorized (frightened, anxious, etc.). While in their state of terror, they pressure their government to change its political outlook in a way that satisfies the goals of the attackers and (most likely) displeases the government and many of its people.

Variation 1 of NPS All is the same as with NPS, except the result is not a change of outlook of the victim government but a weakening of that government. This variation of NPS can come about because the frightened 'innocents' realize that their government cannot protect them. So they lose confidence in it and, perhaps, abandon it in favour of the attackers or their sympathizers.

Variation 2 of NPS All is the same except that the innocents who are terrorized change their behaviour (e.g. by fleeing the country and allowing the attackers to ethnically cleanse it).

Variation 3 of NPS Instead of harming or killing innocents the attackers threaten them. The threatened innocents are terrorized into behaving in accordance with NPS, or Variation 1 or 2.

Variation 4 of NPS The attackers operate under the flag of NPS, or Variation 1 or 2, but do not escape. Instead they become martyrs.

A second narrow version concentrates not on the victims of terrorism but the actors. It says that terrorist actors have to have a non-state status. If one then combines this version of the notion of terrorism with that of attacking only innocents the concept becomes exceedingly narrow but, supposedly, easier to handle. A narrow definition makes it easier to determine whether this group is or is not terrorist in nature. In contrast, broad definitions or characterizations tend to open the door to all sorts of activities designated terrorist. Broad definitions or characterizations, the argument runs, are not just broad, they are loose and unprincipled. We shall investigate these topics further later on.

2 Suicide/Martyr Terrorism

Various kinds of martyrs

The fourth variation of the paradigm scheme in Chapter 1, having to do with suicide/martyr terrorism, deserves special attention. It is deserving not because it is new, for this form of terrorism has a long history. Martyrdom itself has an even longer history. It goes back at least to the days of the Old Testament where Jews would martyr themselves because they refused to worship the gods of others. Later, in the days when Rome was so powerful, the Zealots fortified themselves in the Masada fortress, fought the Romans and, in the end, died by their own hand just as they were about to be overpowered. They were true martyrs. Later, also under Roman rule, many Christians also martyred themselves. They did so in more than one way. Some refused to take oaths of allegiance to Rome; others simply declared their allegiance to Christianity. Still others died in hopeless defence of their religion.

One of the earliest martyr *terrorist* groups was the Assassins. This Islamic group flourished in the eleventh, twelfth and thirteenth centuries. The name 'Assassins' has its roots in the drug hashish that the group is said to have used ritually.[1] The group was much feared, and with good reason. Its members did not fear death: rather, they welcomed it.[2] Working in the name of Allah, and having been promised rewards in the afterlife, death for them was something to look forward to. Further, the Assassins went about their business of killing high officials with great skill and efficiency. Their favourite weapon was the dagger. Upon assassinating the chosen official, the killer would expect to die. And he usually did. Those surrounding and presumably protecting the unfortunate official would either kill the assassin on the spot, or very soon after.

Modern martyr/suicide terrorists

It is not, then, its newness that makes today's suicide/martyr terrorism worthy of special attention. Rather, it is worthy as a growing phenomenon perceived by many to be the most effective of all forms of terrorism. 'Suicide bombing is unique in the sense that the organizations which use this tactic reap multiple benefits on various levels without incurring significant costs.'[3]

In contemporary times, suicide/martyr terrorism was reinvented in the 1980s by Hezbollah. In 1983 its suicide bombers attacked the US embassy, US marine barracks and French paratroop barracks in Lebanon, killing more than 300 civilians and military personnel. The intended secondary result of these bombings was to get the Western military out of Lebanon. In this regard, Hezbollah was successful. President Ronald Reagan and the French government pulled their troops out. Further, in this victory over the West, Hezbollah gained immense prestige. So much so that other groups, the rebel Tamil Tigers in Sri Lanka for one, decided to imitate them. Others who adopted the fourth variation of the PS include rebels from Israel/ Palestine, Chechnya, Afghanistan and, now most especially, Iraq.

Given this new-found popularity of suicide/martyr terrorism, there is a need to ask and answer the following questions.

1. How many forms or kinds of suicide/martyr terrorism are there?
2. How does suicide/martyr terrorism contrast with other forms of terrorism?
3. Which term, 'suicide' or 'martyr' best characterizes this form of terrorism?

Since these questions are intertwined, we will deal with them together rather than separately.

Notice how 'suicide' fits well into any discussion of modern suicide/martyr terrorism. Using a bomb-laden belt or a car filled with explosives, terrorists literally commit suicide by themselves. To be sure, they almost always have help from others by way of justifying the suicide effort and by way of helping make the bomb or belt. But it is they who set off the bombs that lead to their own destruction. No one else is needed to get that job done. This is suicide pure and simple even though the motive for the act is not the kind we normally think of when it comes to suicide. We suppose that people commit suicide out of self-pity or to gain relief from suffering (caused by a disease). Instead, the primary motive for terrorists is to harm and terrorize an enemy.

The Assassin's suicide is suicide once removed. An Assassin terrorist does not kill himself directly. He kills someone else, and is himself killed by another. Nonetheless, we count the Assassin's act as suicide because he knowingly places himself in a position where it is impossible for him to escape with his life.

Actually there is a bit of hesitation in saying that the Assassin has committed suicide. Perhaps in the eleventh century his death, following his assassination act, would be certain. But a modern Assassin might be seized and held in captivity. It depends on who his captors are. However, if the 'assassin' bites down on a cyanide capsule when captured, our hesitation vanishes. He now, without question, earns the title of a suicide terrorist.

But if the assassin knows he might survive and yet, in fact, is killed, it is not clear whether his death would count as a suicide. As his chances of survival go from 5 per cent to 10 per cent to 30 per cent and then to 50 per cent, we increasingly are tempted to say that it was not suicide.

The concept of 'martyrdom' works differently. At first when death is certain, 'martyrdom' tracks 'suicide'. But even when we back off calling a terrorist act suicidal because the chances of survival are significant, the terrorist can be and is often still called a martyr. If the terrorist is fighting for a cause, and if he gives his life for that cause even if it was expected that he would survive, he could still be called a martyr. In some cultures the martyr's cause need not even be religious, and the one killed might not be a terrorist but instead be an ordinary soldier.[4]

In one sense, then, although the concept of martyrdom overlaps that of suicide, it has broader uses. It is so broad in fact that it gives us little or no clue about the nature of the terrorist act. The terrorist could have acted so as to put his life in very great danger, or he could have placed an improvised explosive device on a street at a time when it was carrying no traffic. In the latter case, he might fully expect to return home in a few minutes for some wine and cheese. However, if he is killed (an unmanned aerial vehicle observed his actions) he might be said to have been killed 'by an act of Heaven'. Even so, he still might be counted as one of the martyrs of the cause for which he was fighting.

In contrast, the concept suicide delimits to some extent the actions of terrorists. Very likely they used a belt or car bomb. Or possibly they used an AK-47, all the while carrying a cyanide pill to do themselves in as they are about to be captured. However they perform their suicide acts, these acts are more narrowly circumscribed than are the acts of martyrs.

This circumscribing gives us a clue as to why martyr/suicide terrorism is so popular these days. If bombs are being used, they are smart bombs since they are guided into place by creatures with a human brain. Terrorists could use other smart weapons and not necessarily do something that automatically ends their lives. Mortar- or rocket-propelled grenades are smart weapons in that they can be accurately aimed so as to destroy targets. And terrorists use these weapons in a variety of situations. But there are times when these kinds of weapons cannot be used. It would be difficult, for example, for a female terrorist to carry such weapons into the middle of Tel Aviv. For her purposes, it is better to wear a belt-bomb and so appear pregnant, get on a bus and, when that bus becomes crowded, blow herself and everyone else up. In other situations, bombs can be made smart by placing them in automobiles, vans and trucks, and then driving them into or next to a building, other vehicles or a crowd of people.

Apart from being the weapon of choice in many situations, the modern bomb, compact and powerful as it is, helps make martyr/ suicide terrorism achieve a surprising level of success. As Robert Pape argues,

> Perhaps the most striking aspect of recent suicide terrorist campaigns is that they are associated with gains for the terrorists' political cause about half the time ... of the thirteen suicide terrorist campaigns that were completed during 1980–2003, seven correlate with significant policy changes by the target state toward the terrorists' major political goals. In one case, the terrorists' territorial goals were fully achieved (Hezbollah versus US/F, 1983); in three cases, the terrorists' territorial aims were partly achieved, (Hezbollah versus Israel, 1983–85; Hamas versus Israel, 1984, and Hamas versus Israel, 1994–95; in one case, the target government entered into sovereignty negotiations with the terrorists (LTTE[5] versus Sri Lanka, 1993–94 and 2001; and in one case the terrorist organization's top leader was released from prison (Hamas versus Israel, 1997). Six campaigns did not lead to noticeable concessions (Hezbollah's second effort against Israel in Lebanon, 1985–86); BKI's[6] attacks against Indian leaders in Punjab in 1995; a Hamas campaign in 1996, retaliating for an Israeli assassination; the LTTE versus Sri Lanka, 1995–2002, and both PKK[7] campaigns).[8]

Apart from being a most effective weapons system against an enemy, suicide attacks have another important advantage. They help to shore up morale on the (terrorist) home front. When terrorists first considered using suicide as a tactic, some thought that it would backfire. People, they thought, would be offended by attacks on civilians and by the sacrifice of the suicide attackers. But it turned out just the opposite. The terrorist rhetoric was able to marginalize the victims of suicide attacks. These victims are said to be heretics, apostates, corrupt, corrupting of others, guilty of prior crimes, aggressors, exploiters, etc. in varying combinations. It was, and is, relatively easy to find labels so that their status as human beings is discounted to the point that harming them was, and is, seen as not being morally wrong.

But beyond even that, the status of the suicide attacker is enhanced by terrorist rhetoric.[9] He or she is celebrated. Typically, video pictures are taken of the attacker before the final sacrifice is made. Then, after the attack, the attacker's family is honoured, stories are told about the attacker's high motives, 'playing-cards' with the hero's pictures are distributed to the young, and the hero is praised publicly in the media and (usually) in religious settings. Far from viewing the sacrifice as a way of exploiting the (usually young) attacker, he or she is viewed as someone who has made a noble sacrifice for the society's good.

The net result of terrorist rhetoric is that what is viewed from the outside as a senseless, cruel and immoral act is turned around completely into a high-minded one. Suicide attacks instead of being wholly bad are viewed as wholly good.

Answering questions

In answering the three questions posed earlier in this chapter (see p. 22), we can say the following:

1. There would seem to be two forms of suicide/martyr terrorism. With one, the terrorist pulls the trigger that kills him; with the other, the enemy kills the terrorist who has placed himself in a position where he will (inevitably) be killed.

2. Suicide/martyr terrorism is in many ways much like other forms of terrorism. The immediate effect of all forms of terrorism is, obviously, to terrorize. Also, all forms of terrorism aim to achieve some kind of secondary effect (e.g. political change). However, they

differ as to their means. Terrorists have many means at their disposal to get their terrible work done. Suicide/martyr terrorism represents one or a small cluster of these means. Of all the means available to the terrorists, suicide/martyr terrorism seems to work best in specific situations. It is a very effective killer, and perhaps even more effective as a terrorizing tactic. People and governments tend to worry more about dealing with those terrorists who are not afraid to die. Perhaps they feel this way because they are uncertain as to how to deal with them.

3. The concepts of suicide and martyrdom do not completely overlap. Martyrdom is the broader concept, in that it can be applied to persons who lose their lives for 'the cause' by accident rather than by design. Nevertheless, the two concepts overlap sufficiently to warrant using both terms interchangeably in those terrorist acts where the main actors know with a degree of certainty that they are going to be killed.

3 Cases from the Recent Past

Russian terrorism (c. 1880–1917)

The outbreak of terrorism in Russia at the end of nineteenth and the beginning of the twentieth century is well documented. In the words of Anna Geifman:

> From April 1866, when the former student Dmitri Karakozov made the first unsuccessful attempt on the life of Tsar Alexander II, through July 1918, when Lenin and his closest associate, Iakov Sverdlov, ordered the assassination of Tsar Nicholas II, and soon thereafter proclaimed a general policy of Bolshevik 'red terror', a half century of Russian history was bloodstained by revolutionary terrorism.[1]

The phenomenon of Russian revolutionary terrorism has many causes. One of its roots is found in the ideas of French socialist Blanqui, who was the first to proclaim the possibility of socialism triumphing by means of revolutionary conspiracy. A second root is found in Russian soil. The ideas of Blanqui were further developed by Peter Tkachev and Nikolay Morozov. The first Russian political organization to implement the concept of terror as a road to justice was called the People's Will (1878–81). The People's Will was crushed in the long-run by the police, but its ideas and practices were inherited by the Socialist Revolutionary Party (1901–18). Besides these two classical organizations, there existed dozens of others. They practised terrorism, but did not officially introduce the concept as part of their agenda. The People's Will is thus generally regarded as the first European terrorist organization of the contemporary type and the Socialist Revolutionary (SR) party as a further implementation of the same concept.

Why did Russian society, traditional in many respects, act ahead of its time with respect to terrorism? The answer can be found in the specific process of modernization in Russia. In the late nineteenth century, Russia combined rapid modernization of its economy with a backward political structure and social life. This combination produced many people, who became alienated and frustrated. These people were easily marginalized and so were willingly enlisted in the most militant revolutionary organizations of the day. At the same time, many representatives of the Russian intelligentsia had no political voice, but wanted to move the society in a progressive direction.

P. Tkachev (1844–86) was the first intellectual who proclaimed the idea that the uniqueness of Russian society rests in its rural community, and that socialism can be more readily implemented by means of that community. The only hindrance was the tsarist autocracy that was absolutely marginal to the functioning of the Russian society. Thus, a war should be declared on the tsar and his followers. Since the majority of peasants were still politically somnolent, ignorant and unable to understand their true happiness, the revolutionary party would wage this war on their behalf. One Russian scholar rightly expressed the essence of Tkachev's ideas: 'The dominant idea was: as soon as the autocracy, which has no social support in the Russian society fails, Russian socialism, based on communitarian instincts of the peasants and public property in land will flourish.'[2] N. Morozov (1854–1946) further developed his idea of the just war on the reactionaries. The war should be waged by means of terror. He was confident that 'three or four assassinations of tsars', one immediately following the other, would bring a total collapse of the political system. The power would fall into the hands of the socialists, who would use the state apparatus to introduce socialism, freedom, equality and justice to the society. The terror should be all-embracing. Not a single official should ever be free from the fear of sudden and unpredictable execution. The aim of all this terror was to kill two birds with one stone. The official state would be paralysed, and the masses would be awakened from their slumber.

The People's Will was persistent and successful. Its greatest success was on 1 March 1881, when the carriage of Alexander II was blown up, killing the tsar. The triumph of the People's Will was at the same time its swan-song. The organization was quickly eliminated by the police. There were a number of attempts to revive it, one being made by a group of socialists including Lenin's older brother, Vladimir Ulyanov. He attempted in March 1888 to take the life of Alexander III. This time the revolutionaries did not succeed, and Ulyanov and his companions were hanged by verdict of the Supreme Court.

For about 15 years following the liquidation of the People's Will, there was a pause. But that was the pause before the storm. The real storm of terror followed after 1901, when several socialist organizations managed to unite into one strong, well-heeled and well-organized party of Socialist Revolutionary Party. The SRs proudly considered themselves to be the real spiritual heirs of the legendary People's Will. They were right, but only partly so. True, they revived the tactics of individual terror to an extent undreamed of by their old-fashioned predecessors, but they did not inherit certain moral constraints that were recognized by the People's Will. The People's Will consisted mostly of the members of the privileged classes, who participated in the struggle to achieve high moral goals. The SR party consisted mostly of 'marginals' who were capable of hatred, but hardly capable of moral constraint. As a result, the SR party increasingly put aside the considerations of discrimination and proportionality.

But, in the beginning, the SR party was picturesque and seemed to be a reincarnation of the People's Will. The scope and the extent of terror by the SRs were impressive. Their very first terrorist acts were highly discriminatory. Each official was supposed to be punished for his personal crimes.[3] The first victim was the Minister of Education, N. Bogolepov, in February 1901. He was killed by a former student, Peter Karpovich. In April 1902 came the assassination of the Minister of the Interior, Dmitrii Sipiagin. In July of the same year the chief of Khar'kov police was murdered. In May 1903 the governor of Ufa province was shot. In July 1904 a bomb was tossed into the carriage of the new Minister of the Interior, Pleve, killing him instantly. In February 1905 a large homemade bomb was thrown by Ivan Kaliaev at a member of the imperial family – Grand Duke Sergei Aleksandrovich. The governor-general of Moscow, F. Dubasov, was wounded in April 1906. All told, during a one-year period beginning in October 1905, 3,611 government officials of all ranks were killed and wounded throughout the empire. By the end of 1907, the total number of state officials killed or injured came to 4,500. The peak reached in 1905–06 was never achieved again, but even in calmer periods the extent of terror was still appalling. From the beginning of January 1908 through mid-May 1910, the authorities recorded 19,957 terrorist acts and revolutionary robberies, as a result of which 732 government officials and 3,051 private persons were killed and 1,022 officials and 2,829 private persons wounded. Between 1894 and 1916, close to 17,000 individuals became victims of revolutionary terrorists.[4]

The SRs were well organized and disciplined. Their structure included the Central Committee, responsible mostly for the strategic issues and ideology, and the Combat Organization, dealing strictly with terror. The Combat Organization was only loosely affiliated to the Central Committee and so secretive that even the members of the Central Committee at times doubted its existence. The Combat Organization was comprised of the group of people who made terrorism their life's mission. For them, group affiliation dominated their individual aspirations. The majority of them were Jews, who had severed connections with their ethnic and religious background for the benefit of the revolutionary mission.[5] As a rule, the combatants paid little if any regard to ideology, but many of them were moved by ethical considerations. Thus Fedor Nazarov considered himself an anarchist rather than an SR, but belonged to that movement because it did terrorism better. Abraham Gotz was Kantian; Maria Benevskaya was a zealous Christian; Egor Sazonov was also a Christian. Sazonov possessed a messianic fixation, and was willing to become a martyr. Dora Brilliant possessed no ideology at all. She was a sadistic terrorist who tossed bombs 'just for the hell of it'.

The indiscriminate nature of SR violence was in striking contrast to the practice of the People's Will. Of the 671 employees of the Ministry of the Interior killed or injured by terrorists between October 1905 and the end of April 1906, only 13 held high administrative positions, while the other 658 were city policemen, coachmen and security personnel.[6] In general, wearing a uniform was sufficient to qualify as a potential victim of the terrorists. On many occasions, the bombs were tossed in the midst of military regiments of the Cossack squadrons.

The lack of discrimination and general disregard for human life was not the only moral drawback to the SRs. The moral decline of the terrorists of this new type was evident even to the SRs themselves. Some of them diagnosed the disease as Nechaevism.[7] But it was not only Nechaevism. Nechaev, with all his Machiavellianism, was still an iron revolutionary who was able to give up his life and put aside all personal considerations. The terrorists of the new generation were different. Probably the best exposition of the morality of the brand new terrorists was delivered by the head of the Combat Organization – Boris Savinkov. In the fashionable novel *Pale Horse*[8] (which he published under a pseudonym), his colleagues were depicted as immoral, arrogant, disillusioned and sadistic. The general moral decay typical of Russia at that time contributed much to this specific decay of the terrorist's morality.

The SRs were not the only Russian terrorists at the turn of the century. Terrorist tactics were gradually adopted by Maximalists, anarchists and ordinary criminals. None of them had organizations comparable to the SR party and none openly adopted terror as part of a programme. Nevertheless, they used terror to a greater extent than even the SRs. The level of neglect of the discrimination principle and the lack of concern for the value of human life was even worse than the SRs'. Not surprisingly, their level of moral motivation was much lower. These organizations represented the slippery slope of moral decay. Thus, the Maximalists made an attempt on the life of the prime minister, Arkadii Stolypin, in the most indiscriminate manner without any concern for innocent life. On 12 April 1906 three Maximalists, dressed as gendarmes, slipped into Stolypin's villa during visiting hours and detonated a powerful bomb. About a hundred people were killed or badly wounded, including Stolypin's daughter and son, but Stolypin himself escaped serious harm. On another occasion, a Maximalist armed with a revolver entered a police-occupied private apartment and started to fire randomly. He escaped, leaving several people dead.

The anarchists also appealed to terror. But unlike the SRs and even Maximalists, they lacked any central organization to coordinate their actions. They also had a principled disregard for discipline. Dozens of loosely organized 'Black Banner' units waged terrorist war on their own accord. They usually did not bother to find an appropriate target. Any official they did not like could become a target. Any entrepreneur could become a victim since, following Proudhon, they believed strongly that all 'property is theft'. They acted like racketeers by threatening death to those who refused to pay them. Anna Geifman claims that of 17,000 victims of terrorist activities between 1901 and 1916, the lion's share can be blamed on the anarchists. Indiscriminate violence causing general panic was the very essence of their deeds. According to anarchist theory, that is the road to general anarchy (the mother of order) – to the truly just state of society.

The most notorious among the anarchists were the so-called 'Bezmotivniki' terrorists (motiveless terrorists). They used to cooperate with the lower strata of society, especially thieves. In practice, they did not distinguish themselves from ordinary criminals. In theory, they claimed that their acts of robbery should be regarded as revolutionary activity. It is true that they, unlike the criminals, very often demonstrated personal courage and dedication. Nietzschean supermen served as their model of behaviour.

Some groups of terrorists were of an obscure nature and could be regarded neither as revolutionaries nor bandits, but as a blend of the two. Among them was the legendary Grigorii Kotovskii, who organized a private army of bandits. He used to rob and kill the wealthy landowners and merchants in Bessarabia, but often shared his profits with the poor, Robin Hood-style. After the Bolshevik coup in 1917, he became one of the commanders of the Red Army, but later fell victim to the totalitarian terror of the state. Kotovskii was ignorant of any socialist theory but had a perfect sense of the criminal world, and a taste for luxury, wine and women.

The criminals comprised the seamy side of the Russian revolution. They always cooperated with Russian revolutionary movements of all orientations including Social Democrats and even Liberals. Time and time again, many criminal gangs claimed that they possessed the revolutionary spirit in their willingness to expropriate the unjustly accumulated money of the rich. In Soviet Russia, the Bolsheviks used the service of the thieves' world once again. This time they used them to guard the regime's political opponents kept in the 'Gulag'. These criminals were to inflict terror on the potential political opposition to the regime.

A great number of terrorists were simply psychologically unbalanced. One of the terrorists, by the name of Kamo, who was involved in dozens of terrorist actions alongside the Bolsheviks and was considered one of the heroes of the revolution, was in fact a recorded psychopath. Dmitrii Bogrov (a paid agent of the police), who assassinated Stolypin in 1911, was a suicidal maniac. He committed this terrorist act in order to achieve a more or less honourable death, and to escape death at the hands of his companions. Dozens of terrorists were open sadists, who not only murdered people but also attended their funerals, just for the fun of it.

The moral decay of revolutionary terrorism in Russia became evident in the case of Evno Azef. Azef was a member of the Central Committee of the SRs and coordinated the activity of their Combat Organization. It is well documented that he was a paid agent of the Russian secret police. Terrorism was a successful business for him. Not only did he accept a handsome amount of money from the Russian government, he was also extremely successful in raising money for terrorist groups. As it turned out, he embezzled a great deal of these funds. At the same time, the government was so ill-organized to strike back at the terrorists that police efforts were just a mockery of a real struggle. The weapons and the techniques of the police were both outdated and cumbersome. The prisons resembled clubs, where terrorists could discuss their programmes and tactics, and the Siberian settlements for the political convicts were reminiscent of the resort hotels. In fact, the government went out of its way to assure Europe of its humanitarianism.

In October 1917 the Bolsheviks seized power. The SRs as well as anarchists were willing to continue with their terrorism even after the Bolshevik coup, because the Bolsheviks 'proved to be the traitors to the ideals of freedom who usurped the state'. But this time the terrorists had to face the real terror of the iron fist of a totalitarian state that went far beyond the horrors of tsarism. Individual political terrorism had no chance against the overall terror inflicted by the terrorist state.

Blockades in the First World War

There were two major blockades during the First World War. One was carried out on the sea, the other under the sea. The first was the British naval blockade of Germany, the second the German submarine blockade of Britain.

The British blockade was implemented at a distance.[9] It was safer that way. Had the British moved their blockading fleet close to the European mainland, they would have been vulnerable to attacks from German coastal submarines and from mines. Besides, a distant blockade was just as effective as one 'close in'.

The British blockade was moderately effective in controlling the German fleet. That fleet forayed away from its home ports only occasionally. The only time it ventured out in large numbers was in 1916, and that foray led to the Battle of Jutland.[10] The battle was a tactical victory for Germany. Although both sides suffered losses, the British lost more ships and men than did the Germans.[11] But strategically the Germans gained nothing. Indeed, at Jutland, the German fleet was almost trapped by the British and escaped only by virtue of their excellent seamanship and a good deal of luck. The German fleet would never again risk another fight with the larger and more powerful British fleet.

But bottling up the German navy was only part of the British blockade plan. The blockade was also supposed to keep war materials from reaching Germany. Trading with Germany in such materials would have generated handsome profits for foreign governments and businesses. However, the blockade kept chemicals needed for the production of explosives (e.g. saltpetre, nitrates and nitrogen) from reaching Germany.

Beyond that, the blockade had another purpose. It was meant to keep food supplies from reaching Germany. Normally the Germans could feed themselves. But during the war, farmers became soldiers, and farm horses became war horses. Coupled with the effects of the blockade on the fertilizer supply, German farm production suffered severe losses. The resulting food shortage harmed the military to some extent, but the German government made certain that those who were directly supporting the war effort were given priority status in what food was available. As a result, it was the civilian population that suffered the most. The worst of their suffering took place late in the war. Evidently, the strangling effect of blockades took time.[12] Overall, the blockade probably caused or significantly contributed to the death of over 700,000 German civilians.[13]

The German blockade was quite different from the British. Whereas the British sat back, as it were, and waited for the German war effort to waste away, the Germans aggressively went after British shipping with their submarines (U-boats). They attacked naval, armed merchant, unarmed merchant vessels and even passenger liners indiscriminately. Actually, this policy of indiscriminate or unrestricted submarine warfare was not carried out throughout the whole war. At the beginning, German U-boats mounted surface attacks in accordance with the so-called cruiser rules. These rules mandated giving those on board an attacked merchant vessel time to abandon their ship, and allowing them provisions before their ship was sunk (usually by gun-fire). But, in the long run, these gentlemanly surface attacks proved unfeasible. If they attacked on the surface, the U-boats were themselves vulnerable to attack by naval vessels and by so-called 'Q' ships. 'Q' ships were heavily armed, but also disguised to look like ordinary merchant vessels. The unwary U-boat commander would quickly regret surfacing and then attacking such an innocent-looking ship.

So the U-boats were forced to attack under the sea in order to survive. And for a long while they did. While surviving, they did fearful damage to British shipping. In February of 1917 U-boats sank a total of over 500,000 tons of shipping. In March the numbers went over 600,000 and by April well over 800,000.[14] It was not until late that year, after the British admirals reluctantly accepted the idea of convoys that the numbers began to go down.[15] In the end, the U-boat campaign failed. However, it actually came close to succeeding, and indeed could have succeeded. 'At one time there was less than a month's supply of wheat in England.'[16]

The question to ask about these blockades is: Do they constitute a form of terrorism? On the surface (pun intended), the British blockade does not seem to. The blockade does not target victims who fit the Chapter 1 characterization of terrorism (i.e. any of our paradigm schemes). No one is killed or maimed so that others will be terrorized. The passive nature of the blockade seems to preclude thinking of it as a campaign of terrorism even though it had a terrible effect on the German population. It may even be granted that because of that effect, the campaign was immoral. But the effect of weakening the German population through starvation, immoral as it might be, was not due to terrorism. Rather, the weakening effect was due directly to a blockade that kept food away from the German population. The only possible role for terrorism in this blockade is in the reaction of those neutral countries who wanted to trade with Germany. If they became so intimidated by the blockade that they decided not to trade with Germany, that reaction could be viewed as a form of terrorism.

However, 'intimidation' might not be the right word to characterize neutral reactions here. It may be, and most likely was, more a matter of prudence. Given the blockade and the dangers of trying to run through it, it was prudent to look for markets somewhere else than in central Europe. So the concept of terrorism has little if any role to play in the British blockade even though, as noted already, that blockade failed to meet the standards of the principle of discrimination in just war theory.

A better case for terrorism can be made for the German blockade. This is so not because the blockade represented pure terrorism. Like the British, the German blockade's main purpose was to weaken British resolve. The British were supposed to be discouraged into quitting the war, not terrorized into quitting. But the nature of attacks by a stealthy and deadly instrument of war allows for terrorism to play a role in the submarine campaign as well. 'Neutral and American shipping refused to sail for British ports.'[17] The massive number of sinkings (the victims in our characterization) terrorized, and intimidated others not to take the risk of delivering any kind of goods to Britain.

Bombing of Germany during the Second World War

After the fall of France in the summer of 1940, Britain faced the might of the German military machine alone. During this period, it was not obvious that Britain would survive. German submarines took a heavy toll of British shipping, and the Luftwaffe almost overwhelmed the Royal Air Force (RAF) in its attacks on British airfields. In the end, Britain did survive. But in fighting alone, it had no weapons with which to seriously harm Germany. The British fleet was intact, and it did successfully blockade Germany. But a blockade of an expanded Germany that had access, for example, to Romanian oil products could not even come close to bringing Germany to its knees. As to the British army, it too could do little to harm Germany. It was badly mauled during the fall of France and survived (without most of its equipment) mainly because of the miraculous rescue at Dunkirk. During this period, it did fight General Erwin Rommel and his Africa Korps in Libya and Egypt, but even there the British often could barely hold their own let alone overwhelm the Germans (and Italians). As to the RAF, it too was in no position to harm the Germans in any significant way. Its fighter command was spent as a result of the Battle of Britain, and its bombers at that time were woefully inadequate to do much damage either to German industry or its war machine.

However, there was a way open to the British even if they had to face their enemy alone. During the First World War and afterwards some British military leaders came to look with favour on the idea of mounting a strategic bombing campaign against any future enemy.[18] These thinkers were not necessarily against developing weapons and skills for fighting a tactical war. They agreed that an air arm should be capable of supporting the troops as they moved against an enemy on the ground. But strategic bombing of enemy facilities far behind the lines was thought also to be needed. Some supporters of strategic bombing believed that this new way of fighting could actually be decisive. It might win the war all by itself. Not all were that sanguine, but many influential British political and military leaders were convinced that strategic bombing could have such a significant effect on the outcome of a modern war as to make the development of large bombers worth the effort.

What was needed by way of flying machines were bombers larger and more modern that the two-engine Wellingtons – the best British bomber available when the war started. Interestingly enough, the United States, but neither Germany nor France, nor even Russia, felt the need to have such large bombers. The Americans had developed their four-engine B-17 well before they entered the war. In turn, once the war started and once the inadequacies of the planes the British had in hand became clear, they too got into the business of producing large bombers. The most successful of these, the Avro 683 Lancaster, saw the light of day in 1941.[19] By the time a good number of these, and other less capable four-engine planes (the Halifax and the Stirling) became available, the British had learned about the high cost of daylight bombing. They had also learned that night-time bombing could be highly inaccurate. At first, the British thought that they could bomb small oil-plants to some effect at night. That proved unfeasible. Then they decided that their night bombers might go after larger targets such as railway yards, but that too proved unworkable. The Butt Report of July 1941 claimed that during British attacks on the Ruhr, only one in ten bombers got within five miles of the target.[20]

Matters improved when the British developed radar-based navigational aids such as Gee, Oboe and H_2S, and target-indicator bombs.[21] But even with these new devices, the RAF simply could not achieve enough accuracy to attack small or even medium-sized targets. The new aids got them to the target with greater frequency, but to be located the targets had to be cities or very large towns. Put simply, the British had the choice of using their new bombers on urban areas, or of reversing the decision to build their strategic bombers since there would be few military uses for them.

It is important to appreciate what the British did not know as these bombers came on line. They did not know about the difficulties they would encounter in finding and attacking distant targets. After all, the concept of strategic bombing was new to everyone – not just to the British. Advocates of strategic bombing were optimistic and exuberant about the new technology. Others were more sceptical. However, those who prevailed in getting the heavy-bomber programme started genuinely believed that these bombers could be used to do serious damage to the enemy's military-industrial complex. They persisted in this belief in part because of faulty intelligence. Early on in the war (1940 and into 1941) photographic results of the bombings were generally not available. So the RAF relied on crew reports to determine how much damage was done to the enemy. These reports turned out to be overly optimistic by a wide margin.[22] In the meantime, the commitment had been made to build large bombers and to train thousands of young men to fly in them. At the time, it seemed like a good decision.

The bombing campaign built up slowly. Not all the bombers were aiming at German cities. But Berlin was bombed early during the 1940 Battle of Britain, in part in order to avenge the German bombing of London. The following year, the build-up was barely underway. It is true that by then the British were no longer alone. The USSR had been attacked in June. But in a sense that made matters worse since that year the German campaign against the USSR (Barbarossa) was very successful. The Russians pleaded with the British to make a contribution toward slowing the German advance as it was moving toward Moscow, Leningrad and Stalingrad.

By 1942 more large bombers came onstream. This made the first 1,000 bomber raid (on Cologne) possible. In that year as well, the Americans joined the fray. They said that they intended to bomb in daylight and to focus their attacks on military and military-supporting targets. The British saw no reason to change their night-time bombing policies. In fact, they had no choice. Their new large bombers were not suited to daylight bombing. They simply were not fast enough, nor did they carry enough guns, to defend themselves against the high-quality German fighter planes they were facing.

As still more bombers and crews to fly them became available in 1943, the raids on German cities became bigger and more frequent. By 1944 and 1945, Bomber Command's terror bombing campaign was in full stride. Here is Stephen A. Garrett's account of what all this bombing accomplished during these years.

> As a method of warfare, 'area bombing' focused not on specific military or industrial targets but rather on German cities themselves. The targeting instructions given to British aircrews indeed typically designated the center of such cities as the prime 'aiming point.' The RAF launched some 390,000 sorties against Germany in the entire course of the war, and the area attacks accounted for about 70 percent of the total effort, with approximately one million tons of bombs being dropped on the enemy. By the end of 1944 about 80 percent of all German urban centers with populations of more than 100,000 had been devastated or seriously damaged. This exercise in destruction continued even into the spring of 1945, with almost 40 percent of British bombing being directed at city targets. It is *estimated* that overall some 500,000 German civilians lost their lives as the result of the area offensive, and perhaps another 1,000,000 received serious injury. Around three million homes were destroyed.[23]

In short, the RAF bombing campaign represented state terrorism against another state on a massive scale.

Kamikaze

If terrorism is, in part, defined as attacks on 'innocents' (civilians, non-combatants, those not directly involved in a war, etc.), then the Japanese use of suicide warfare in the Second World War cannot be thought of as an example of terrorism. After all, Japan's suicide programmes were aimed at Allied (mostly American) military personnel and machines. However, our characterization of terrorism is broader in scope. It allows that certain government officials, police and even military personnel can be terrorized. It is possible, then, for these programmes to count as examples of terrorism. Is, then, the use of suicide by the Japanese in the Second World War an example of terrorism?

There is a long tradition of suicide in Japanese culture. The person who has behaved disgracefully in almost any social setting is expected to commit suicide (*seppuku*). So also is the officer who disagrees with important decisions made by his superiors. If, for example, an officer is ordered to stop his troops from fighting (as at the end of the Second World War), and he disagrees with that order, he can obey his superior and yet express his disagreement by committing suicide. Also, suicide among the military is the preferred option to surrender. Officers either kill themselves directly or, with their comrades, commit suicide in a mad *banzai* charge against enemy lines.

These kinds of suicide were common throughout the Second World War. However, as the war began to go badly for Japan, the high command realized that something had to be done to stem the tide of the Allied advance. One suggestion was to establish a special attack group of air pilots and their machines. This group would not fight the Americans in direct air-to-air combat. By 1944 it had become painfully clear to the Japanese that as American aeroplanes and air personnel improved, Japanese losses were becoming prohibitively high. Instead of engaging in dog-fights, what each member of the special group would do is crash his plane into some high-value US navy ship such as an aircraft carrier, battleship, cruiser or troop ship. Desperate times required desperate measures.

The new group, called kamikaze (divine wind),[24] was formed late in 1944 (officially on 20 October).[25] The group was first used against the Americans in their attempt to retake the Philippines. But the full force of the kamikaze attacks was felt on and around Okinawa the following year. American marines landed on that island on 1 April

1945. Typically, the planes designated to attack in kamikaze fashion were flown by pilots who were not especially well trained. They would fly together in small groups, being escorted to their targets by better-trained pilots. By smashing their planes into enemy ships, the hope was that the Okinawa invasion would be stopped. Failing that, the hope was that the cost of the invasion would be so high as to deter the Americans from invading the Japanese mainland.

The aeroplane kamikazes were not the only suicide weapon that the Japanese employed in the Okinawa campaign. They also employed *baka* (idiot) bombs. The Japanese called them *ohka* (cherry blossom) bombs. These weapons were rocket-propelled. Because they had a short range, they had to be carried by a large plane to an area near the target before they were released.[26] Surface ships were also used as suicide weapons. Indeed, in the battle of the East China Sea, the Japanese sacrificed their super-battleship *Yamato*.[27] This beautiful and powerful ship was supposed to steam to the American landing-zones at Okinawa and, with its 18.1-inch guns, cause as much havoc as possible. It never got close to the landing-zones as it was sunk by swarms of carrier-based American planes. The Japanese suicide weapon arsenal also included mini-submarines as well as small fast-moving naval craft. But it was the aeroplane that did most of the damage. And the damage was considerable. Thirty-six American ships (many of them destroyers) were sunk in Okinawa campaign and 368 damaged (including many carriers). The death-toll was 4,900, with a further 4,824 sailors wounded.[28]

Again, not all of this damage and these casualties were caused by Japan's suicide weapons since mines and ordinary bombs took their toll as well. But it was obvious to both the Japanese and the Americans that the suicide tactic was extremely effective. American military commanders were in shock as to what was happening. How, they wondered, could so much damage be done to the American navy *after* the Japanese navy had been destroyed? Moreover, the suicide tactic affected the morale of the sailors. The thought of a kamikaze aeroplane aiming straight at your ship, and perhaps aiming directly at your station on the ship, induced terror on a large scale.

There was, then, a terrorist aspect to these attacks. But terrorizing sailors seemed to have been a secondary consideration in the minds of the Japanese. What was primary was stopping or slowing the American juggernaut.[29] Making thousands of Japanese pilots and sailors martyrs was, then, mostly a means of war toward that end. These martyrs destroyed and damaged great numbers of enemy ships because they unerringly guided their bombs to their targets. Put differently, these martyrs made their bombs 'smart' at a time when 'smart' bombs were still half a century away from being invented.

The Provisional Irish Republican Army (PIRA)

In 1921, after years of revolt and killing, Ireland became an independent state. It did so as the result of the Anglo-Irish Treaty. Of the 32 Irish counties, 26 became what was to be called the Irish Free State. However, six of the counties (in what was to become Northern Ireland) with a high proportion of Protestant citizens remained part of Britain. The partition was not popular with certain Catholics in the Irish community. In their view, the treaty imposed on the Irish people by the British created two illegitimate states. For them, the Provisional Government (proclaimed as early as 1916) of all of Ireland was the true Irish state.

The unease between those who favoured union and those who favoured separation was present from the beginning. This tended to flare up into violence when one side and then the other sponsored demonstrations affirming their religious and ethnic identities. In 1969 one such demonstration sponsored by the Apprentice Boys (Orangemen) of Londonderry proved to be the match that set Northern Ireland on fire. Counter-demonstrations and rioting followed. Over a thousand police attempted to quell the rioting, and eventually contingents of the British army arrived. In that year the Provisional IRA (PIRA) was formed. The Provisionals (in contrast to those who belonged to the less radical Official IRA) led the way in the direction of more violence to help the cause of unification. Various Protestant groups did their part to keep the violence going. The result was a low-intensity guerrilla war that waxed and waned over the years. One of the high (low?) points in this struggle occurred in Derry on 30 January 1972 (Bloody Sunday). On that day, British paratroopers killed 13 Catholic street demonstrators.[30] Soon after, the Provisionals responded with a series of bombings in Belfast (Bloody Friday).

The Provisionals' targets included British police and military forces, famous personages (e.g. Lord Louis Mountbatten,[31] killed on 27 August 1979), powerful political figures (e.g. Margaret Thatcher and John Major, prime ministers during the last decades of the twentieth century, were attacked but not killed), various Protestant leaders in Northern Ireland, suspected traitors of the PIRA cause, criminals and even ordinary people.[32] They also targeted financial institutions and government buildings in an attempt to destabilize the government of Northern Ireland. Their favourite weapon was the bomb. This helps to explain why 'civilian' casualties were higher than one might suppose they should be. In the process of attacking a bank, for example, civilians would be expected to die in their role as collateral damage. Yet, at other times, 'civilians' were attacked directly.

In the course of their campaign, PIRA considered using martyr bombers. But this campaign never really got off the ground. Apparently, it received little support from some those who sympathized with PIRA and the majority of the Catholic Irish population. Some were repelled by the idea. Another kind of martyrdom, that of the hunger-striker, was better received:

> PIRA prisoners had political status removed from them after 1977. In response, over 500 prisoners refused to wash or to wear prison clothes …This activity culminated in the 1981 Irish Hunger Strike, when 9 IRA … members starved themselves to death in pursuit of political status. One hunger striker (Bobby Sands) and Anti-H-Block activist Owen Carron were

elected to the British Parliament and two other hunger strikers to the Irish Dail. In addition, there were work stoppages and large demonstrations all over Ireland in sympathy with the hunger strikers. Over 100,000 people attended the funeral of Bobby Sands, the first hunger striker to die.[33]

Although this off-and-on struggle has been rightly called a guerrilla war, terrorist tactics were in evidence from the beginning. PIRA's goal was not just to weaken its various enemies militarily but to frighten them into submission. It was, for PIRA, a war of terror designed to create a demand by the British people to withdraw its forces from Northern Ireland and thus lead the way toward unifying Ireland.[34] In the end, the campaign failed.[35] It is difficult to know why. It may be that the more brutal its killing policies became, the more the general Irish population turned against PIRA. PIRA conceived of its campaign against the British as one of attrition. It wanted to wear them down. What evidently happened is that its own people were worn down first. They tired of PIRA's violence before the British became so discouraged by that violence that they quit the struggle.

By way of gaining perspective, it should be noted that, as the result of PIRA activities, fewer than 4,000 individuals lost their lives during the whole struggle.[36] Perhaps heavy mass-media coverage made these losses seem greater than they in fact were. In spite of numerous individual acts of cruelty, both sides showed a measure of restraint, so that the struggle in Ireland never became more than a low-intensity affair. One needs to compare these figures with those of guerrilla/terror campaigns in Armenia (see Chapter 5) and Darfur (see Chapter 4), among other places, where the death-toll ran into hundreds of thousands.

Aceh

Aceh (Acheh, Atjeh, Achin) is located at the northern tip of the island of Sumatra. The waterways that surround Aceh are the Indian Ocean to the west and north, and the Strait of Malacca to the east. Aceh converted to Islam in the eighth century as that religion began to move east. Its strategic location made it the entry door for Islam in that part of the world.[37] Aceh's strategic location also made it possible for it to become a military power that generated influence on mainland Asia where Malaysia and Thailand now are.[38] The religious conviction of the Acehnese people, their military prowess and their long history of running their own affairs made them fiercely independent. It is not surprising, therefore, that they resisted pressure from the Dutch as that colonial power tried to extend its already considerable influence in south-east Asia into the remote regions of Aceh.

The Dutch began to think about annexing Aceh into their colonial orbit late in the nineteenth century. A businessman, W.H. Read, who also served as a part-time Dutch counsel-general, convinced the Dutch in 1873 that they had better move quickly to take over Aceh before other colonial powers (e.g. the United States, Italy) beat them to the punch.[39] Occupying Aceh seemed not too difficult since civil strife had weakened the local government in recent years. But what looked easy to do was not easy at all.

At first, the Dutch moved clumsily in their takeover bid. Rather than patiently negotiate with the Acehnese, the Dutch bombarded some fortifications near the capital, Banda Aceh, and later sent an ill-prepared invasion force to complete the occupation. After some bitter fighting, the Dutch were turned back. During the fighting the Dutch leader, Major-General J.H.R. Kohler, was killed.[40]

The next Dutch attempt was larger and better organized. Eventually, after losing many men to fighting and disease, the Dutch could claim victory. But it was only a partial victory because, although they claimed to have won over the whole nation, in fact they only succeeded in occupying a number of forts and some towns. The countryside was outside the realm of their real authority. What followed was a guerrilla war, one that was waged in the jungle and the mountains of Aceh. It was a double guerrilla war. The

Acehnese conducted raids and ambushes, as did the Dutch. The intent on both sides seems to have been not only to grind down the enemy, but also to terrorize them into submission. The victims of all this fighting were not only combatants but innocent villagers and Acehnese who were not sympathetic to the colonizers. In this extended guerrilla war, the Dutch gradually gained the upper hand. Evidently, they were more systematically ruthless than their opposition. By the first decade of the twentieth century the Dutch claimed victory.

But in fact the rebellion continued even if on a smaller scale. It also changed in character. The Acehnese began to think of their rebellion in more religious terms. It became a holy war. With this change of character, there came an increase in suicide attacks.

> In 1912 the KNIL [the Royal Netherlands Indies Army] lost fewer than one hundred killed in Aceh, and the war was finally considered ended, although spontaneous guerrilla outbursts and suicide attacks continued until the Japanese invasion of 1942. The suicide attackers typically hurled themselves at unsuspecting Dutch victims with sword or dagger, seeking to do as much damage as possible before they themselves were cut down. The Dutch banned the 'Song of the Holy War', which glorified suicide in the cause of resistance … Nevertheless, there were 162 suicide attacks on KNIL personnel and Dutch civilians between 1910 and 1938.[41]

Once the Dutch abandoned their empire in the area, and Indonesia gained its independence in 1943, Aceh's troubles did not cease. The central government in Jakarta was keen on bringing in all the islands and all the regions in the larger islands under its authority. The Acehnese people resented the high-handed policies of the Jakarta government. They had hoped for independence with the departure of the Dutch. Instead, they had acquired new masters.

In the early years of Indonesian independence, the Jakarta government promised Aceh more autonomy. But it failed to deliver on its promises.[42] Soon, and not unexpectedly, a rebel movement demanding independence began to take shape. It called itself the

Free Aceh Movement (Gerakin Aceh Merdeka, or GAM). It is reported that it received funds from Libya and Iran. As it geared up its operations, GAM attacked police stations and police personnel, and military personnel and facilities. It also attacked natural gas facilities. The Acehnese felt that the central government was not giving them a fair return of the abundant natural gas found within its borders. GAM also attacked civilians that it perceived were opposed to its grand plan of independence. In effect GAM was fighting both a guerrilla war and a war of terror.

The government's response to GAM was brutal.[43] The Indonesian military killed thousands and forced many to leave the province. It too was fighting a guerrilla war, and a war of terror. Over the years, many ceasefires were signed and then broken. After a last round of attacks and killings, on 15 August 2005, GAM and the Indonesian government signed 'a comprehensive peace accord'. The signing took place against the backdrop of the 2004 tsunami that killed as many as 200,000 Acehnese, and created a serious homelessness problem for over 400,000. Evidently both GAM and the government were too busy dealing with the catastrophe to continue their struggle. As the result of the accord, GAM allegedly disarmed and the government pulled most of its troops out of Aceh (except for some locals). As of the end of 2006, the peace accord seems to be holding, but only time will tell whether it really will hold.

Greek terrorism

In Greece, terrorist organizations made their debut in 1974 during the period of dictatorship.[44] Following the fall of the dictatorship regime, two terrorist organizations came to light: Revolutionary Popular Fight (ELA) in 1974 and the Revolutionary Organization 17 November in 1975. These two organizations shaped their thinking so that their tactics and ideologies remained stable throughout their operations.

Both organizations placed themselves on the left of the political spectrum without being tied to any parliamentary groups. However, their left-wing political beliefs were obvious from the proclamations that followed their terrorist actions. Not surprisingly, the government intelligence services were constantly looking at left-wing non-parliamentary groups in order to identify those who were participating in terrorist activities.[45]

With regard to whether these organizations thought of themselves as terrorists, it is worth looking at one of 17 November's statements, which proclaimed that the organization's aim was not to create fear among the general population, but rather to target those who had acted against the popular interest and the rights of the people. Those assassinated by 17 November were chosen for their unjust actions. Because only the guilty were targeted, 17 November said that the people should not be afraid of the organization's activities. Furthermore, 17 November claimed that the guiding reason for the organization's existence was to protect the interest of the people, and make those who did not serve that interest pay for their actions.[46]

While denying that they are terrorists, both 17 November and ELA, in fact, shared characteristics found in many other terrorist organizations around the world.[47] More specifically they shared the following properties:

- They had a concrete structure and had established ways for taking collective decisions.
- The role of each member in the organization was discrete. No two members did the same job, and each member was clearly aware of his duties and how to fulfil them.
- There was leadership giving generic guidelines for the acts of the organization. The leader was thought to have a dominant role in deciding what moves the group was to take. He suggested targets that the other members, in consultation with the leader, accepted.

- The organization (and its members) took full responsibility for its actions.
- There was absolute secrecy in the organization's hierarchy.
- The process of recruiting new members was highly secretive. So much so that anti-terrorist squads could not disrupt the organization's operations.
- Access to crucial information about the organization's operations was limited. Thus, if one member of the group was arrested, he was not in a position to give away much information, even if he wished to cooperate with the state.

Targets were very carefully selected so that they could be justified beyond question. Further, watching the moves of the target was a way of safeguarding against mistakes. The rationale behind the target selection was explained by a proclamation, in which violence was presented as the only way of resisting a state that was not functioning in the best interest of its people.

The targets of these organizations can be divided into three types:

- ex-partners of the dictatorship regime, especially those who took part in torture against people who resisted the regime;
- US citizens (as the United States was thought to be actively opposed to Greece and the Greek interests);
- entrepreneurs who violated the law with respect to their relationships with their employees and in how they dealt with the state.

Up until about 1980, target choice for both organizations showed a preference for US citizens. This preference, running in parallel with the anti-American marches, was an expression of great discomfort and anger for the part that the United States played during the dictatorship and for its polices in the Cyprus issue.

In the operational field, there was an important factor that separated ELA from 17 November. ELA worked with explosives on buildings, while 17 November targeted and killed humans.

During the 1980s, target choice began to take on social and political meaning. Both organizations showed more interest in targets coming from the political or business spectrum and correspondingly less interest in American targets. During this same period, there were numerous small-scale bombings of state buildings. But people were targeted as well. Finally, there was the theft of rockets and other weapons. This theft, from an army camp, was credited to 17 November. It marked a milestone in strategy since it significantly enhanced that group's operational abilities.

From 1990 on, the choice of targets, especially in the case of 17 November, was in reaction to social, political and financial events. The bombing actions, the assassinations, the use of rockets that started in that decade did not result in any strong reaction from the state for a number of years.

In what follows, we discuss the most important acts of each of these organizations.

ELA

ELA began its activities in 1975. It either bombed buildings or set them on fire, or it attacked vehicles. Its main targets were

- industrial buildings especially of multinational foreign organizations (though there were exceptions here) and
- vehicles of foreign diplomats in Greece (mainly in 1975, 1977, 1980, 1981, 1982, 1985, 1991, 1992, 1994).

These targets remained constant throughout the lifetime of ELA. In 1977, as a result of attacking AEG facilities, Chr. Kassimis, a member of the terrorist group, was killed, and two other people were injured.

In parallel, the terrorists looked at targets with an aim of causing harm to the government and exposing various weaknesses of police forces. There were attacks against the Communication Department of the Metropolitan Police and the Army House in 1977, a police car in 1979, the offices of the Greek Tourist Organization in Syntagma

Square in 1980, three police cars in 1981, numerous police cars in 1985, the City Hall of Athens and a Metropolitan Police Station in 1986, the State Accounts Department, the police station in Vyronas, a building of the Inland Revenue, the buildings of the ministries of Agriculture and Finance in 1987, the central administration building of the European Community, another Inland Revenue building and Peiraias Metropolitan Police Station in 1988. Beyond that, the Ministries of Health and Justice were bombed, as well as another police station in 1989, the Ministry of Finance in 1990, the Police Special Forces building in 1991 and 1992, the European Community Administration building in 1994, and so on.

Other attacks took place on buildings that were either used by foreign diplomats or which contributed to the acquaintance of Greeks with the language and culture of foreign countries (e.g. the attack against the home of the American ambassador in 1982, the US military base, as well as the embassy of Germany in 1985, the UN building in Athens in 1991, the embassy of Belgium, the Goethe Institute and the French Language Institute in 1994).

In addition, ELA attacked banks and other foreign-capital organizations (e.g. American Express, Siemens and the Coca-Cola Company in 1976; American Express, Bosch and BAIW in 1997; American Express again in 1978; IBM, Honeywell and Honeywell–Bull, Amcor, American Express and the Chase Manhattan Bank in 1982; Alico and Interamerican in 1991).

Finally, there were some targets the choice of which cannot be easily explained, as the main users of these buildings were ordinary citizens (e.g. the arson of cinemas Attikon and Kallithea in 1977; the arson of public transport buses in 1979; refrigerator lorries and tank cars in 1980; as well as the planting of explosives in a Greek-owned supermarket in 1982 and the bombing of night-clubs in 1988 and 1992).

ELA was active mainly in the period between 1974 and 1985. It wasn't until the beginning of 2003, however, that the first three suspects were questioned. Soon after, the Attorney-General began prosecution proceedings against Aggeletos Kanas, Costas Agapiou and Eirini Aggelaki. They were accused of joining and participating in a terrorist organization. In the trial that followed the three were found guilty, but they appealed against the decision and the new trial is still in process.

17 November

As we have noted, the main difference between 17 November and ELA is that 17 November always chose human targets, thereby giving its actions a strong political and social flavour. The first assassination took place in 1975, and the victim was Richard Welsh, chief officer of the CIA in Greece. Terrorists took full responsibility for their action with two proclamations that justified the shooting. According to the proclamation, Welsh was in charge of a whole network of local, well-paid, agents.[48] Almost a year later, Evangelos Mallios was shot dead. He had been dishonourably discharged from the Greek police force for torturing prisoners during the dictatorship of the Colonels.[49] A few years later, in January of 1980, Pantelis Petrou, a high-ranked police officer was assassinated. The attack on Petrou resulted in the death of his driver Sotirios Stamoulis as well. Three years later George Tsantes, chief of the US military force in Greece, was assassinated. His driver, N. Veloutsos, was also killed. In April 1984, another attempt was made (fortunately with no success) to kill American airman Robert Chand.

From 1985 onwards, the organization stopped targeting US citizens. The first victim of the 'new era' was N. Momferatos (February 1985), the publisher of the daily newspaper *Apogeumatini*. A few months later, a van transporting officers of the Special Police Forces was bombed. An officer was killed and many were injured. A year later, the entrepreneur and factory owner D. Aggelopoulos was killed. The next victims were the surgeon Zach. Kapsalakis (February 1987), A. Athanasiadis (March 1988), chief executive of the Bodosaki Foundation,[50] and the American naval officer, Captain Bill Nordeen

(July 1988). In 1989 the prosecuting attorneys C. Androulidakis and P. Tarasoyleas were targeted in an unsuccessful attack. All these attacks were part of the 'purgation process' that the terrorists had announced.[51] In the aftermath of the financial and political Koskotas scandal, an investigation was undertaken by the parliament and civil courts to find guilty politicians and to take them to court. During this period, terrorists made an unsuccessful attempt against George Petsos – ex-Minister of Public Order. A few months later Pavlos Bakogiannis, a member of the Greek Parliament, was killed (September 1989).

In 1990 an unsuccessful attempt was made against businessman V. Vardinogiannis with the use of rockets that were stolen the year before from the Sykoyrio military camp. In 1991 a bombing attack was launched against the American sergeant Ronald Stewart, while in 1992 terrorists attacked the Minister of Finance, I. Palaiokrassas, with a rocket. This attack resulted in the death of Arxarlian, the first civilian casualty of 17 November's campaign. Arxarlian's death was regretted, but justified by 17 November as an inevitable consequence of a war against a corrupt state.[52] The same year an attack was made against E. Papadimitriou, a member of the Greek parliament. In 1994 17 November attempted to kill M. Vranopoulos and, later, a Turkish diplomat. In the following years, there were attacks using rockets against the home of the German ambassador, as well as against the organization's 'favourite' target, the American embassy in Greece.

In 2000 a new era started with the assassination of British military attaché Stephen Saunders. This brought in the British intelligence services and led to cooperation between the British and Greek intelligence services, as well as with the Greek police force, to uncover those behind 17 November. This led to the arrest of Alexandros Giotopoulos, head of the organization, in 2002, as well as other members.[53] The arrests started from a random incident in June 2002. The accidental explosion of a time-bomb device in the hands of Savvas Ksiros, a member of the terrorist group, led to the discovery and arrest of those who had been managing multiple terrorist attacks for over 20 years. The activities of the group stopped and a trial followed.

In conclusion, we note that Greek terrorism in the second half of the twentieth century was an important example of civil terrorism. The main targets were either individuals or places that were associated with government activity contrary to the interests of the people. Especially for 17 November, the 'professionalism' it exhibited in its targeting resulted in very few civilian casualties. The terrorists considered themselves saviours of the nation, and their ultimate target was to 'clean up' political and public life. They aimed to correct all wrongdoing in public affairs. In foreign affairs, they opposed the American influence on Greece, which they saw as not in the interest of the country and its citizens.

In their targeting policies and pronouncements, the terrorists made it clear that the public was not their target, and so should not worry. Those whom they pursued they saw as having betrayed the interests of Greek people. Thus they 'punished' their victims for their actions *pour encourager les autres*.

4 Contemporary Cases

Sri Lanka

Sri Lanka is a divided country. In the north and east the people are mainly Tamils, and their religion is Hinduism. In the rest of the country the people are Sinhalese. Their religion is Buddhism[1] and numerically they are the dominant people. However, historically, they were not dominant in business, education and in the government. The Sinhalese claim that this was so because their British colonial masters favoured the Tamils. The Tamils say their high socioeconomic status is due to merit. Whatever the case, things began to change after the collapse of the British empire brought liberation to Sri Lanka (formerly Ceylon). Now the numerically dominant Sinhalese passed laws favouring themselves rather than the Tamils. The most important of these laws was the Sinhala Only Act of 1956.[2] That act made Sinhala the official language of the country and it became difficult, and sometimes impossible, for any non-Sinhalese speaker to hold certain government jobs. The act also changed university admissions policies to favour Sinhalese over Tamil students. These policy changes did not sit well with the Tamils.

By the 1970s relations between the Tamils and the Sinhalese had gone from bad to worse. The government encouraged a 'land grab' policy that displaced many Tamils from their homes and lands[3] and a political party called the Tamil United Liberation Front (TULF) was both outlawed and denied seats in the Sri Lankan parliament. But worst of all were the events that took place in July 1983. By that time, protests against government policies had moved beyond simple demonstrations and passive resistance. Younger Tamils began to resort to violence, and people were killed. One such act of violence led to the death of 13 soldiers.[4] The perpetrators were members of a group calling itself the Liberation Tigers of Tamil Eelam (LTTE). As a response, riots broke out in the capital city of Columbo at which more than a thousand Tamils died. Others fled in terror. These riots came to be called the Black July Pogrom.

The violence continued after the pogrom, even though efforts were made to bring about a peace agreement. By 1987 there was a further escalation of violence. By then, both sides were setting off bombs in urban centres that inevitably resulted in the death of civilians. But in July of that same year, the violence took a new turn. An LTTE member by the name of Captain Miller, who also belonged to a smaller group calling itself the Black Tigers, drove a truck full of explosives into a Sri Lankan army camp. He killed himself and 40 soldiers. The inspiration for this bombing seems to have come from Lebanon. (In 1983 Hezbollah's bombing of the US marine barracks killed 241 marines and encouraged President Reagan to withdraw US military forces from Lebanon.) Similar episodes followed, but the bombings were not restricted to military targets. Banks, businesses, shopping centres, and Buddhist shrines all came under attack. Not surprisingly, many innocent civilians lost their lives. By the year 2006, perhaps as many as a hundred suicide bombers had done their work. Until the war in Iraq began in 2003, this represented the largest number of such bombers worldwide.

The bombers did not just kill those who happened to be at the wrong place at the wrong time. On two occasions their targets were major political leaders. The background to the first of these 'events' had to do with the role of India in the Sri Lankan conflict. In the 1980s India had sent a peacekeeping force to Sri Lanka. The Tamils welcomed the force composed mainly of fellow Hindus. So did the Sinhalese. The Sinhalese saw the Indian Peace-Keeping Force (IPKF) as an instrument to help restore order in Tamil country. Indeed, the Indian prime minister, Rajiv Gandhi, helped broker a peace accord in 1987. Unfortunately, the accord did not hold, and, in time, the Indian military overstayed its welcome. Opposition to the Indians increased dramatically. Indian soldiers were said not to be treating the Tamil civilian population well, and there were charges of killing, looting and rape. One victim of rape from the city of Jaffna became a Black Tigress and plotted revenge. Her name was Thenmuli Rajaratnam (aka Dhanu). Evidently, she was acting not only on her own behalf (and of her four brothers who had been killed by Indian soldiers) but also on behalf of other victims. Whatever her exact motives, on 21 May 1991 she put on her suicide belt (a new device at that time for the LTTE and the Tigers) and then went to attend a political rally. Here is Pape's account of what happened.

> The plan was simple. According to accomplices and messages captured after the attack, the LTTE sent a squad of assassins to Madras, the largest city in the southern Tamil Nadu region of India, about three weeks before. Rajiv Gandhi [now an ex-Prime Minister but running for office again] was scheduled to speak at a major political rally. Dhanu was the designated assassin. It was her job to wear the belt bomb, carry a garland for Gandhi, 'accidentally' drop it at his feet, bend over to pick it up and explode the bomb at the precise moment when Gandhi (and she) would receive its full force.[5]

The plan worked. One of her accomplices took pictures of the event, showing Dhanu smiling just before the bomb went off. (In fact the accomplice got too close to the explosion and so he too was killed.) The second political leader to die as the result of LTTE action was none other than the Sri Lankan president, Ranasinghe Premadasa. He was killed on 11 May 1993 when his motorcade was intercepted by a suicide bomber on a bicycle. Thirty-four other people died in the bombing. The bomber was thought to be a 14-year-old girl.[6]

Other targets of LTTE attacks included Sri Lankan generals, a Sri Lankan opposition (political) leader, various government officials, policemen, military personnel, a Red Cross ship (which was blown up), bus passengers, shoppers, villagers and farmers. It seemed that no one viewed as unsympathetic to the LTTE cause was immune.

The LTTE mode of attack varied. In addition to employing suicide bombers (both male and female, and mainly young), it engaged in 'ordinary' terror attacks, guerrilla-style warfare and even in conventional military skirmishes. The conventional fighting it did in the past was against the Sri Lankan and the Indian military. These same two military groups were also targets of the guerrilla battles LTTE fought. As to 'ordinary' terror attacks, the targets included other rebel groups who dared to challenge LTTE's position as the leader of the rebel cause.

In order to carry out all these operations, LTTE needed (and needs) a source of funds and other support. For a time, it received help from the Indian government. Another source was the Indian state of Tamil Nadu where, understandably, the LTTE has many sympathizers. Money from that part of India and other parts of the world where Tamils live came, to some extent, freely. But the LTTE was not above pressuring, and even threatening, those whom they thought should be giving money but were not. But the main source of funds has been illegal drugs – mostly heroin.[7] The movement of drugs starts in Sri Lanka and India and goes from there to Turkey, to various European countries, to Canada and to the United States. Over the years, hundreds, and by now probably over a thousand cases of trafficking have been reported to Interpol.

The weapons which LTTE buys with its money come from many sources. Some of the main ones are Singapore, India (especially from the state of Tamil Nadu), Afghanistan, Pakistan and the Middle East.

At the time of writing, the LTTE and the Sri Lankan government are actively killing and maiming one another. Those attacked, whether they be Sinhalese or Tamils, are often non-combatants. And so it goes on.

Chechen terrorism

The two main causes of Chechen terrorism are Chechen separatism and Islamic radicalism. The Chechens claim for independence led to the first Russian–Chechen war of 1994–96. That in turn, led to the outbreak of the second war in September 1999, which then led to the Russian control over the territory. However, guerrilla acts are still occurring.

At the very beginning of the separatist war in December 1994, the influence of Islam was relatively small. The leader of the rebel Chechen republic, the former Soviet general Johar Dudajev, had very few if any Islamic grievances. His idea was to set up an independent secular state similar to the several Baltic states which already had gained independence from the former USSR. The Chechens, in general, although they are Muslims, have never been radical or zealous. Besides, their understanding of Islam is not orthodox since their religious beliefs have much to do with prehistoric pagan traditions.

The war that the Chechen rebels fought at the very beginning was rather clean in terms of *jus in bello* norms and practices. The Chechens honoured the principles of discrimination and proportion-ality, and their attitude to prisoners of war was reasonably humane. But in the course of war, and after suffering heavy casualties and several defeats, the rebels gradually began to employ terrorist tactics. To some extent, this was a rational response. The rebels could not hope to defeat the powerful Russian army in regular field operations. Further, they thought that their terrorist tactics would put pressure on the weak and corrupt Russian government of Boris Yeltsin. Last, but not least, what might seem to be terrorist tactics were in fact often acts of revenge. These acts were not centrally planned, but were carried out by the members of this or that clan against Russian soldiers in general, or some particular unit, responsible for the death of a certain Chechen individual. The Russian indiscriminate artillery and aviation fire produced heavy casualties among civilians. For the

Chechens, with their traditions of blood revenge, acts of individual terror seemed to be the only way to gain revenge. All of these considerations, no doubt, contributed to the launching of the first terrorist attack on Budenovsk by the Chechen rebels led by Shamil Basayev.[8]

The Chechen attack in June 1995 was shocking. About a hundred fighters emerged out of the blue in that peaceful town in southern Russia. Within a few hours, they rounded up hundreds of people and herded them in to the local hospital. All together, the Chechens held about 5,000 hostages. It was the largest hostage-taking in history. They mined the hospital entrances and put their fighters with machine-guns in defensive positions. The fighters hid behind the sick, pregnant women, doctors and children. The attack of the Russian troops went ahead, but when the hostages were forced by the Chechens to stand in the windows, wave white sheets and scream, it stopped. After the second storming failed, Prime Minister Viktor Chernomyrdin personally began to negotiate. There would be a ceasefire in Chechnya and Basayev's men would be allowed to escape. True to their word, the Russians signed a ceasefire accord on 21 June. This time the successful terrorist tactics saved the Chechens from defeat. Almost the same scenario was staged by the other warlord Salman Radujev in Pervomaiskoye in January 1996 not far from Chechnya. But this time, although the Chechens took several hundred hostages, the Russian military attacked and did not negotiate.

It is fair to say that the first Chechen war was lost by the ill-trained and poorly led Russian army. By the end of 1996 an armistice was signed, on terms next to Russian capitulation. But the *de facto* independent Chechnya which won the war failed to win the peace. The total collapse of its economy, endemic corruption of the government, banditry and lawlessness turned out to be the features of Chechen postwar social life.

Soon, the ideas of radical Islam started to infiltrate Chechen society. The new leaders of the Chechen republic became confident that they would never find support in the West. But radical Islamists, including al-Qaeda and the Taliban, were ready to give support. In return, they wanted Chechnya to become a militant Islamic republic. The ideology of Wahhabism (an eighteenth-century traditional Islamic movement) started to spread over the republic and was adopted by the most powerful warlords, including Basayev. At the same time, motifs of Chechen greatness and messianic Islamism coexisted with the expansionist idea of a liberated single 'Caucasian home', or 'Caucasian confederation'. These ideas became very popular.[9] As a result, Chechnya was officially proclaimed an Islamic state in 1998.

But at this point the Chechen society split. The majority of ordinary Chechens and Chechen religious leaders, unlike the new warlord elite, did not want to confront Russia in another war; nor did they not want to adopt Wahhabism as a state religion.[10] They were sick of the instability and devastation caused by the earlier wars. Further, some of the Chechens became pessimistic about the notion of gaining independent status. It seemed evident to them that one clan or another would always rule an independent Chechnya, and that clan would be the sole beneficiary of the country's independent status.

Nevertheless, the radicalization of Chechnya continued. The militant Islamists intended to continue the war with Russia in their goal of creating the Islamic Republic of North Caucasus. In reaching this goal, terrorism was a high priority in their plans. Early in 1999 several apartment buildings were blown up in the Russian cities of Buinaksk and Moscow. The plan was to demoralize and frighten the Russians. Soon after that, the Chechen Islamic radicals crossed the border and invaded the neighbouring Russian republic of Dagestan. As a result, the second Russian–Chechen war started in May 1999. Keeping to their priorities, terrorism became one of the militants' major tactics in this war. The official Chechen propaganda threatened all kinds of terror on Russian society including the devastation of nuclear power plants and chemical factories.[11] But this time, both Russian society and the Russian army reacted differently. The society supported the government in a programme to put down the rebels, and the army was better equipped and organized. In September 1999 the new Russian president Vladimir Putin ordered a military assault on Chechen strongholds. By spring 2000, Chechnya was occupied by the federal troops. But guerrilla actions continued.

The terrorism of the Chechen guerrillas had two main targets. It was aimed at those Chechens, who supported the official govern-ment backed by the Russians, and it was aimed at the Russian public. A considerable number of Chechen officials fell victim to the Islamic radicals. The most successful terrorist act of this sort was the assassination of the new Chechen president, Akhmad-Hadji Kadyrov. This assassination of the Kremlin's handpicked Chechen president dealt a severe blow to federal plans. But, this time, the Chechen Islamists miscalculated. They made the same mistake the Russians made in the first campaign. They did not take into account the traditions of vendetta still in place in Chechen society. As soon as a member of a clan is murdered, he has to be avenged. The acts of terrorism against the Russian-backed officials led to retaliations and from there into a general vendetta of the clans. Both Russian-backed and al-Qaeda-backed clans were exposed to full-scale terrorist tactics against each other. Both sides took hostages and killed people at random. In effect, the war turned into one for the domination of the republic.

The other side of this terrorism was directed against the general public all over Russia. These acts were well subsidized by al-Qaeda. For many Chechen rebels, al-Qaeda was their only source of money. One of the most massive terrorist acts of this sort was the raid on Moscow 'Nord-Ost' Theatre on 23–26 October 2002. The fighters emerged during the performance. They took hostages, and threatened to blow up the whole building if their demands were not met. But this time the special police were quick and resolute. A paralysing gas was used and, as a result, all the fighters were shot dead.

During this raid, and on many other occasions, the terrorists engaged in suicide bombings. Some of these bombings were innovative in their use of women as bombers. These women were called the Black Widows. The Black Widows were supposed to be Chechen women whose husbands had fallen in the war. These female martyrs seemed to be not only efficient killers but also terrifying symbols of death incarnate. They made the Russian public tremble. About two dozen Black Widow attacks are recorded, mostly in Moscow, which resulted in the loss of several hundred lives.

The Black Widow phenomenon has been studied by Russian psychologists, including Professor Krasnov. He writes:

> Ideologists of Chechen separatism try hard to create and promote the image of a desperate widow, avenging her husband's death. But in practice most of the young women suicide terrorists are not widows. However, it is true that often some of their both close and distant relatives, have died or disappeared. This is important in the development of a psychological readiness to terrorist actions, but alone is probably not sufficient. What is also needed is for these immediate or recent losses to be linked with the long term ethnocultural perception that these are insults that require a response, invariably a violent response, in other words revenge.[12]

In more detail, the path of the Black Widows is as follows. Young women experiencing a psychological crisis or protracted frustration leading to depression are isolated by older mentors from outward contacts. They are moved to remote villages, exposed to an environment of multiple religious rituals, endless reading of *suras*, and persistent repetition of the theme of revenge on the enemy. In time, these women become increasingly submissive to their mentors. After all that comes practical training in the mechanics of suicide terrorism, such as learning how to use weapons and explosives, and how to navigate through the target city of the terrorist operation. The last stage of training typically takes place close to the intended place of operation. No doubt some of these women have lost family members to Russian atrocities. Possibly some of them have been raped. One of them captured in Chechnya was certainly pregnant. But the training and conditioning they undergo ensures that whatever grievances they have are channelled into potential martyrdom.

The last notable act of Chechen terrorism was the Beslan school hostage crisis (also referred to as the Beslan massacre). In September 2004, armed Muslim terrorists took more than 1,200 school children and adults hostage in the Russian town of Beslan in north Ossetia. This time the terrorists could not manage the hostage-taking. On the third day, a general panic occurred among the hostages. The Chechens started shooting at random and the police were forced to intervene. The loss of life was heavy. According to official data, 344 civilians were killed – 186 of them children – and hundreds more wounded. The notorious Chechen warlord Shamil Basayev claimed responsibility for the hostage-taking.

The attack on the Beslan school seemed to be more 'terrorism of despair' than anything else. Apparently the idea was not so much to terrorize the public as to provoke a revenge response of the Ossetia nation aimed at the neighbouring Ingush nation (many terrorists were Ingush nationals). In turn, all this was supposed to explode the fragile peace in the Caucasus by provoking war between Ingush and Ossetins. This did not happen. What did happen was that the civilized world lost any sympathy it might have had for the Chechen freedom-fighters. Their image was now far more negative than it had been previously.

Terrorism in the Holy Land

Terrorism in Palestine grew out of a typical conflict between settlers and natives. The first Jewish settlers started to arrive in their spiritual Motherland as early as the 1880s. The movement and ideology that stood behind the settlement is called Zionism.[13] Like all the rest of the ideologies of the modernity, Zionism wears a substantial birthmark from the French Revolution: namely, terrorism.[14] But Zionism is not strictly speaking a secular ideology. It is deeply rooted in the history and eschatology of the Jewish religion. Thus the origins of Jewish terrorism can be traced to the ancient religious terrorism of Jewish zealots. God himself, after all, promised to terrorize all the enemies of the Chosen People.[15] In the case of Zionism, terrorism was apparently unavoidable for one very simple reason. There seemed to be no other way to cleanse the densely populated land of Palestine of the natives and so make room for settlers. As Bregman frankly states in his book: 'While there was no explicit decision by the Jewish leadership to expel the Palestinians, there was nevertheless a tacit agreement that this should be done.'[16]

At the time of the first and second *aliyah* or immigration to Palestine (1880–1913), terrorism was not a part of the agenda for two reasons. First, the Jews were a small minority (about 55,000). Had they used violence, they would have been swept away by the Arab majority. Second, Ottoman Turk rule was harsh and autocratic, and would have probably responded by resorting to genocide. The situation changed after the Turks lost control of Palestine and the British assumed the mandate. British rule was beneficial to the Jewish immigrants,[17] and the Jewish population increased to almost half a million between the two world wars. By 1947 there were 608,230 Jews in Palestine compared with about 1,364,330 Arabs.

Apparently, British rule was beneficial to Jewish terrorism as well. The first terrorist groups emerged in the 1930s. One of these organizations was the Irgun Zvai Leumi, headed by Menachim Begin, a future prime minister of Israel. The second was Lochamai Herut Yisrael, known also as Lehi, or the Stern Gang. These were the first classic terrorist organizations of the Middle East. The founders were mainly Russian emigrants. Both the Irgun and the Sternists used the tactics of terrorizing the British administration *en masse*. They also terrorized the Arabs, who were getting increasingly nervous about the Jewish influx. One of the most notorious acts of terror occurred on 22 July 1946 with the explosion in the southern wing of the King David Hotel in Jerusalem, a hotel that the British used as their headquarters. The casualty toll was high: a total of 91 killed and 45 injured.

Eventually, because of these pressures and their sympathy for the plight of the many Jewish refugees, the British decided to bring the problem of Palestine to the United Nations. On 29 November 1947 the UN General Assembly voted to recommend the partition of Palestine into a Jewish and an Arab state. The Arabs would not accept the partition plan. They were adamant that they had a right to the whole of the country, and regarded the invasion of the Jews as nothing more than a new crusade.

A civil war started almost immediately, and this was followed by the war of the new state of Israel with all of the neighbouring Arab states. The generals of the Jewish forces devised what became known as 'Plan Dalet', which ordered the expulsion of Arab inhabitants.[18] The Arab response was violent. Just to give one example: on 31 December 1947, taking revenge for the killing of six of their fellows by the Irgun, Arabs attacked and killed 39 Jews at the Haifa oil refinery.

The Jews won their first war and, in the process, managed to conquer portions of the territory allocated to the Palestinian state. The remainder of the territory came to be ruled by Egypt (the Gaza Strip) and Jordan (the West Bank).

The war led to the creation of the Palestinian refugee camps in the Gaza Strip, the West Bank of the River Jordan, as well as in almost all the Arab states. Some of the results of the war were the feelings of humiliation and revenge shared among the Arabs. These feelings led to the beginning of the *fedayeen* infiltration into Israeli territories.

The early Arab terrorism was of a different nature from the more calculated terrorism of the settlers. Arab terrorism was deeply rooted in the emotions of fear, humiliation, revenge and dismay. Slowly the *fedayeens* became better organized and worked out an ideology of their own. Something like a vicious circle of terror started to emerge.

In their attempt to force Israel to give up the territory captured in the War of Independence and to return to the borders of the partition plan, the Arabs planned to terrorize the population into leaving Israel. Through shellings, direct physical attacks and *fedayeen* infiltrations, the Arabs inflicted 1,300 casualties on Israelis between the wars of 1948 and 1967.

To counter Palestinian violence, the Israelis devised a policy of retaliatory action. Early in 1953, Ariel Sharon formed a special Unit 101. The members wore no badges and carried weapons that were not regular issue for the Israeli military. The purpose was to create 'plausible deniability' so that it could be claimed that the members of this unit were civilians. In the first major raid on 14 October 1953, Israeli commandos dynamited an entire Jordanian village at Kibya to the ground. Sixty-six civilians were killed, most of them women and children, and 75 were wounded.[19] The vicious circle of violence was never broken. Bregman writes:

> Israel's retaliatory doctrine neither curbed infiltration nor eased public insecurity. In fact it achieved precisely the opposite effect for, by reacting massively and disproportionately to even minor Palestinian provocations, the Israeli leadership instilled in the public a mistaken impression that a big and continuous war was being waged between Israeli troops and the fedayeen.[20]

In June 1967 Israel carried out a pre-emptive attack against Egypt, Jordan and Syria, as well as *fedayeen* organizations supported by these countries.[21] Israel conquered the Sinai peninsula, the West Bank and the Golan Heights. By the end of the so-called Six-Day War, Israel had conquered territory more than three times the size of the area it originally controlled. Israel now ruled three-quarters of a million hostile Palestinians. The war of 1967, and the war of attrition that continued up to 1972, changed the entire situation with respect to terrorism. By that time, the Palestinian fighters organized themselves into several groups, with the Palestinian Liberation Organization (PLO) playing the leading role.

The PLO was created in May 1964 by Arab states who wished to supplant the State of Israel by a secular democratic Palestinian State. There were many factions within the PLO, but it soon became dominated by al-Fatah, the resistance organization led by Yasser Arafat.[22] After 1967, the PLO increasingly chose to attack Israeli targets outside the Middle East in order to gain the attention of the whole world. The raids were designed to provoke Israeli retaliation and, eventually, a war with the Arab states that would result in the liberation of Palestine. Supplementing these raids, Arafat's *fedayeen* rivals embarked on a strategy of international terror, including aeroplane hijackings and placing bombs on airliners. The most militant of the PLO organizations was Black September. It burst on the international scene on 28 November 1971, with the murder of the Jordanian prime minister Wasfi Tel in Cairo. In May 1972 Black September attacked its first Israeli target by hijacking a Sabena airliner. On 5 September 1972 a group of eight Black September terrorists attacked the Israeli quarters in the Olympic village in Munich. On 1 March 1973, a group of seven Black September terrorists took over the Saudi embassy in Khartoum, Sudan, where a reception was being held. In Cyprus, Black September murdered an Israeli businessman, attempted to assassinate the Israeli ambassador and tried to attack an Israeli 'Arkia' airliner. An Italian clerk working at the El Al office in Rome was shot dead, and letter-bombs were sent both to American and Israeli targets. From October 1972 to October 1973, Mossad[23] and Black September fought each other across Europe. Simultaneously, the Israelis adopted harsh policies toward the guerrillas in the occupied territories.[24]

As a result of Mossad's campaign, and the failure of the guerrilla war in the occupied territories, Arafat decided to disband Black September and concentrate on attacking targets in Israel from Lebanon. In 1982 Israel responded in her usual manner with massive attacks on those foreign lands that were hosting the terrorists. For two months the Israeli army battered the PLO in Lebanon. The result was the end of the mainstream PLO's military operations in Lebanon.

It was during this war that one of the most notorious acts of state terrorism happened. In September 1982 the Phalangists, who were allied with the Israelis, massacred the residents of the refugee camps in Sabra and Shatila. Various estimates suggest a death-toll of 1,000–2,000 people. It was during this war that martyr terrorism emerged. One of the first suicide attacks on the Israeli army barracks took place on 11 November 1982. Forty-seven soldiers were killed and 27 were reported missing. 1n 1985 a 17-year-old girl called Sana Mhaydli launched a suicide attack on an Israeli patrol. These attacks were also directed against the troops that were summoned to mediate the conflict. On 23 October 1983 truck-bombs were driven into a building where American Marines and French forces were based, killing 241 Americans and 80 other victims. The martyrs belonged to religious (Hezbollah, Islamic Jihad, Hamas) as well as secular parties, including the Lebanese Communist Party.

In 1985 the first intifada started in the occupied territories of the West Bank and Gaza Strip. Intifada was never planned by anyone. It burst out of the blue as an expression of humiliation and despair of the Arab population. Its aim was to instil a sense of national pride and identity in Palestinian youth. But intifada also had its terrorist component. A number of terrorist organizations swiftly adjusted their tactics within the intifada. They also took into consideration the growing rejection of the world public opinion to international terrorism. So this time they switched mostly to a form of domestic terrorism directed strictly against the Jewish population.

The terrorists vehemently rejected the accusation that they were waging an unjust, indiscriminate war. They pointed out that, according to Israeli law, almost every citizen is supposed to be a soldier and so is not protected by the non-combatant principle.[25]

The intifada, and especially its martyr-terrorist component, shocked and split Israeli society. But the Palestinian leadership also came to realize that the attempts to exterminate Israel were an exercise in futility. In 1988 the PLO leader Yasser Arafat renounced terrorism, and the PLO officially recognized the State of Israel.

In 1993 the Israelis started negotiations with the Palestinian leadership on the status of occupied territories of the Gaza Strip and the West Bank. This immediately infuriated the Jewish radicals and led to terrorist acts on their side. Thus on 25 February 1994 an Israeli extremist, Baruch Goldstein, opened fire on the Muslim worshippers, killing 29 before committing suicide.[26] The aim of the attack was to provoke a response, and indeed it did. The Islamic radical organization Hamas bombed a bus in northern Israel on 6 April. Islamic Jihad attacked a group of soldiers at a bus stop. And on 13 April Hamas bombed a bus in Hadera. The three attacks together killed 14 people and wounded 80.

Nevertheless, in early May 1994, Israeli–Palestinian negotiations culminated in the signing of the Gaza–Jericho agreement. In that same month, Yasser Arafat returned to the Gaza Strip to establish the Palestinian Authority. This laid out a timetable for the withdrawal of Israeli troops from those two areas and established the framework for Palestinian self-rule. But autonomy did not stop Arab terrorism. In January 1995, a suicide bomber killed 21 Israelis, and a few months later, more died in a bus bombing. It soon became evident that Arafat simply had no power to control the Muslim extremists affiliated to Islamic Jihad and Hamas. The very nature of Islamic terrorist organizations started to shift after 1993.

The second intifada began in October 2000. It led to a different form of terrorism. The demise of the Soviet Union and the emergence of al-Qaeda led to the general change of the goals of Islamic radicals. The liberation of Palestine was no longer considered to be a goal in itself. The radicals bid higher. They were aiming at a world Muslim *umma*, and the destruction of Israel came to be just one of the minor goals.

Terrorist attacks were now waged on Israel from Lebanon by *fedayeen* units, as well as from Palestine by means of suicide bombers. This was a new kind of martyrdom compared to that of the first intifada. Economic decline and endemic corruption of the patrimonial political elites gave birth to what Khosrokhavar calls a 'schizoid society'.

The second [intifada] was increasingly marked by a pessimistic worldview which more or less implicitly admitted that the nation could not be built. At this point, a holy death that both guaranteed the martyr a place in Paradise and destroyed part of Israeli society became the only tenable solution. It was this political impasse that gave rise to a new form of radical martyrdom amongst the Palestinian *shebab* ('young people'), as well as in other sectors of the population that had not been directly involved during the earlier period.[27]

Radicalization and despair are two factors driving young people to martyrdom in increasing numbers. According to Israeli security sources, Palestinians carried out 42 suicide bombings between 1993 and 2000. Between January 2001 and 5 April 2002 there were 64. Terrorism in the Holy Land does not seem to be fading away.

Darfur

Sudan is bordered just south of Egypt and Libya, east of Chad, and south-west and west of Ethiopia and Eritrea respectively. Sudan is also just north of Uganda and Kenya. Also, part of its eastern border touches the Red Sea. It is one of the largest countries in Africa and, paradoxically, both one of the richest and the poorest. It is the former because there is much oil within its borders. As a result, the good life is available in the Sudanese capital of Khartoum, among other places.[28] But, to the west, in Darfur, poverty reigns. The people living in that region of Sudan are mostly Islamic, as are the majority of those living on the eastern side. But an important difference is that most people in Darfur are of African origin, while the majority of those living in the eastern areas are of Arab descent.

The poverty in Darfur is longstanding and endemic. During the colonial period, the British had little interest in improving the life of the people in Darfur, but things did not improve when they left. The Arab-controlled government continued to neglect Darfur. Hospitals, schools, roads and bridges were few and far between. Understandably, the people of Darfur began to complain about the neglect. Occasionally some of them turned to violence when, apparently, their complaints were not heard. They wanted a more equitable distribution of their nation's wealth. What they got instead was a disproportionate negative response. Instead of help, they got the Janjaweed: a mixed bag of non-regular army forces that do the dirty work that the regulars are reluctant to do. Nicholas Kristoff describes the situation:

> In Darfur, the cleavages between the Janjaweed and their victims tend to be threefold. First, the Janjaweed and the Sudanese government leaders are Arabs and their victims in Darfur are members of several non-Arab African tribes, particularly the Zaghawa, Fur, and Masalit. Second, the killers are frequently lighter-skinned, and they routinely use racial epithets about the 'blacks' they are killing and raping. Third, the Janjaweed are often nomadic herdsmen, and the tribes they attack are usually settled farmers, so the conflict also reflects the age-old tension between herders and farmers.[29]

The people of Darfur began to have trouble with the Janjaweed in the late twentieth century. But it was not until 2003 that the Sudanese government unleashed the full force of the Janjaweed in response to rebel attacks on military and government facilities. Many of these rebel attacks had been quite successful not only in defeating Sudanese army forces but also in taking prisoners and capturing guns and other military equipment.[30]

In response, the Janjaweed, reinforced by criminals released from prison and supplied by military equipment provided by the Sudanese government, adopted what can best be described as a scorched-earth policy. They killed, raped and burned their way across the land. The attacks were discriminatory. African villages were attacked, but Arab villages were not. Those villages seemingly in line of being attacked were terrorized. As many as two million fled their homes, many of them moving into Chad. Others were not so lucky. It is estimated that as many as 400,000 died in the struggle, either as the direct result of Janjaweed attacks or because of starvation and disease.[31] The following description gives a sense of what it was like to live through or die in a Janjaweed attack.

> Thirty-two villages and hamlets along Wadi Deberei were burned – among them Bindisi, Arwala, Sindu and Nankose – and displaced villagers packed into the once prosperous market town of Deleig. Over a period of weeks 172 people were captured and killed in Deleig. Many had their throats cut and their bodies thrown in the stagnant pools of a seasonal river just south of the town. The burning continued. On 5 March 2004, the frightened community around Wadi Debarei woke up to find a wide area surrounded by soldiers and *Janjawiid* who began going from shelter to shelter and hut to hut, asking each man for his home village. Armed with a list of 200 names of 'SLA [Sudan Liberation Army] leaders' drawn up by a local intelligence chief, Ibrahim Jumaa, security officers took away 100 men – almost all of them displaced. In the evening 71 of them – the 'SLA leaders' – were put in army trucks and taken from the police station to a wadi, where they were lined up, forced to kneel and shot in the back of the head. A similar massacre took place in the Mukjar area further south. In all, at least 145 men were executed in Deleig and Mukjar that night. Another 58 were killed in the Deleig area the following day.[32]

Although the Janjaweed were (are) the main killing instruments, government forces were by no means completely innocent.

> Army officers, air force pilots and militia commanders operated in an ethics free zone, as they had in earlier wars. A government official who fled to Switzerland, traumatized by what he had witnessed in the Nuba mountains, said the orders given to the government forces there had been 'to kill anything that is alive. That is to say: to kill anybody, to destroy the area, to implement a scorched earth policy … so that nothing can exist there. In the oilfields the orders were identical: "If you see a village, you burn that village. If you see a civilian, you kill that civilian, if you find a cow, that cow is your cow."'[33]

As this last sentence indicates the Janjaweed and the Sudanese military are not only engaged in killing but also in looting. Fighting for a noble cause is evidently not foremost in their minds. Perhaps

this helps to explain why martyr terrorism has not as yet become a
tactic in the war in Darfur.

Transnational terrorism

By 'transnational terrorism' we understand the terrorism of al-Qaeda
and some other less notable groups. This type of terrorism did not
burst on the international scene, as one might think, because of the
spectacular events of 11 September 2001 (9/11). On the contrary, it
crawled in with the help of American and Soviet secret services, each
of which was breeding terrorists in support of its cause in the Cold
War. By the end of that war, this terrorism was already standing firmly
on its own feet, and could not be easily eliminated by means of the
secret services or even large-scale military operations. The genie had
been let out of the bottle and was not willing to go back in. Some
scholars have already distinguished this form of terrorism as a new
type. It has been called post-classical terrorism, global terrorism,
radical Islamic terrorism, religious terrorism and hyperterrorism.
Rather than play the game of arguing which name is most
appropriate, we are content to distinguish some specific characteristics of this new form of terrorism. Classical terrorism, which we have
encountered so far in this and the previous chapters, was by and
large terrorism of closely knit organizations of zealots (sometimes of
states) pursuing the rational goals of national liberation or ideology,
or both. The enemy was a government or a group (sometimes a
nation). But transnational terrorism is different. Khosrokhavar
describes it thus:

> This type of activism, which some call hyperterrorism, differs from classical
> terrorism. It has no overriding political purpose. It does not attack political
> entities and is not intended to challenge a politically defined order. It is
> directed against the world as a whole, as symbolized by the United States,
> although countries such as France, England, Spain or Saudi Arabia may be
> its actual targets.[34]

Indeed, transnational terrorism pursues vague goals. One is the creation of a neo-*umma*, or community of Muslims all over the world. The contemporary world, even in the most tolerant countries, is hostile to the True Religion. The believers are harassed and their religious feelings are insulted constantly by the very way in which Western societies are organized. The consumption of goods and commodities has replaced the worship of Allah in these countries. The basic features of the West such as sexual depravity, arrogance, tolerance of evil and hubris are aimed at undermining and destroying Islam. The true believers, living in Islamic countries, cannot help feeling humiliated by proxy. The radical Islamic apprehension of religion is exclusive and monopolistic; it is not subject to the relativism of Christianity. The crisis of multiculturalism is closely related to the goal of neo-*umma*. There are certain cultures that simply cannot dwell peacefully inside their shell. They strive to encompass the whole world. Christianity also had such ambitions, but it gradually left the public domain in favour of individual salvation. But radical Islam has not yet put aside its ambitions to dominate the public sphere. Peaceful Islam of private religiosity is regarded by radical Islamists as something different from the true religion of Allah.

The political goal is a caliphate – Islamic government for the whole world or at least for the Islamic countries of the Middle East.[35] It goes without saying that both *umma* and caliphate are regarded as the only way to revive the Islamic religion, which is suffering from widespread idolatry and ignorance even in Muslim countries. Thus Wahhabism sees its duty as squeezing out all the contemporary heretical teachings that are spread throughout the Islamic world.

According to this way of thinking, jihad[36] is the only way to achieve these goals. Since the grievances of Islam are many, and the war on Islam has been waged for a long time by the Satanic West (headed by the United States), jihad should be waged in absolute terms with no limitations as to the means employed. Total terror is one of these means, and so is permitted. Among Islam's grievances are the creation of Israel, the deployment of American troops in the Holy Land of Saudi Arabia, the occupation of Iraq and Afghanistan, the support of corrupt pseudo-Muslim governments, and the harassment of the Islamic religion in the West.

Unlike the classical terrorist organizations of modernity, al-Qaeda is a loose association of small autonomous groups and individuals. It has nothing to do with a classic pyramid structure and hierarchy. It has no headquarters and it is not affiliated with this or that state or region. Members of the group are highly mobile. They come together for specific actions and then vanish. The group's vanguard comes from the upper or middle classes, both from Islamic countries and the West.

One of the essential features of the new terrorism is privatization. Financing for al-Qaeda does not come from any governmental or state funds, as is often the case with terrorism. It is financed by charitable foundations, wealthy individuals, the drug trade, extortion, illegal sales of cigarettes and other goods, or by taking Western hostages (e.g. Abu Sayaf's group in the Philippines specializes in this practice).

Taking into consideration the vagueness of its aims, looseness of structure and the special way of financing, terrorism is destined to play a much more substantial role in al-Qaeda-type terrorism in comparison with any classic form of terrorism. Terror becomes a major binding device for bringing together the scores of semi-autonomous units. It becomes the source of publicity and fund-raising. In general, terrorist activity almost becomes an end in itself. The very notion of a legitimate target disappears. Almost any target becomes legitimate, even fellow Muslims. Fear must be inflicted on all and at every moment. No one is innocent. Everyone is guilty for participating in ungodly practices. From the point of view of Islamic radicals, the West has no individual face or identity and is nothing but a satanic totality. And if some innocents die in the terrorist attack, Allah will bestow a rich recompense on them.

It is no surprise, then, that martyr terrorism has become the core of this type of terrorism. Martyrdom is as old as terror. It is also no surprise that in al-Qaeda's case, martyr terrorism is extremely important. Al-Qaeda martyr terrorism is above all a message, which may be read as follows:

> We are going to fight to the death. Unlike you, the unbelievers, we have no fear of death and are willing to die, because life has no value if it is deprived of real religious sense. But each of us martyrs, heading to Heaven, will be accompanied by hundreds of unbelievers heading to Hell. So you had better think about this, and succumb to the will of Allah.[37]

Historically, al-Qaeda was organized in the 1980s as a result of the war Islamic volunteers (the Mujahadeen) were waging on the pro-Soviet regime in Afghanistan. The military training camps financed by the American government and some Islamic states served as melting-pots for a new Islamic International. The so-called Afghan battalion is still the rank-and-file core of al-Qaeda. Later, other groups and individuals were added to it. Among them were radical Islamic organizations from Palestine, Pakistan, Lebanon, Libya, as well as from Europe and America.[38] On 26 February 1993, an al-Qaeda group demolished three basements of the World Trade Center. Six people were killed and over a thousand wounded. This was the first known al-Qaeda attack against America. There followed attacks on the American air base in Dharan on 22 June 1996 and on the US Embassy in Nairobi on 8 August 1998. The destruction of the twin towers of Manhattan's World Trade Center on 11 September 2001 marked the beginning of a new era and the end of the post-Cold War era.

Al-Qaeda is not the only Islamic terrorist organization of the new type. Hizb-al-Tahrir, operating in Central Asia as well as in some Western countries is another example. One more group is the Harakat al Jahad-al-Islami. This group has close links with Pakistan and operates in Kashmir. It is active in Bangladesh, Chechnya, Uzbekistan, Tajikistan and Xinjang in China.

Islamic transnational post-classic terrorism is the strongest, but in no way only kind. The Aum cult, which released poison gas into the Tokyo Underground on 20 March 1995 in order to terrorize the ungodly society; the Solar Temple, which committed collective suicide in October 1994; and the Seventh-Day Adventists led by David Koresh – all provide the examples of the same logic of unlimited war against the hostile world of unbelievers.

War in Iraq (2003)

The invasion of Iraq began on 19 March 2003. By the 9 April, American forces were in Baghdad in strength, so they could be witness to and participate in the toppling of Saddam Hussein's statue in Firdos Square. The military campaign went well in spite of being hampered by Turkey's refusal to allow the 4th Infantry division to attack Iraq from the north.[39] Starting in Kuwait, the main American military effort moved over 300 miles from south to north within three weeks. Their quick movement kept Iraqi forces off balance. In the south, around Basra, the British moved more cautiously. Even so, by the end of the first week of April, they had occupied that city. In effect, the war to overthrow Saddam's regime was over by the middle of April. The cost in lives to the Americans was 122. For the British it was 33.[40]

However, one early indication that not all was well for the invaders was that the war produced very few prisoners. Some Iraqi units fought, suffered casualties and yielded prisoners, but many simply melted away. Soldiers left the field of battle, carried their weapons and ammunition with them, took off their uniforms, and then went home. Thus, after the Saddam government collapsed and the Americans officially disbanded the Iraqi military, there were many armed and unemployed Iraqis ready to cause problems not only for the Americans and the British but also for those Iraqis who cooperated with the invading forces.

Another early sign of trouble was looting. Even before the fight to overthrow Saddam was over, looters were raiding government and business offices for computers, telephones, copper wire, furniture and just about everything else that could be carried away. More ominously, the looters found that they could access ammunition dumps that the Iraqi military had abandoned, and the 'liberating' forces were not guarding. It quickly became clear that although the Americans and their British allies had brought with them enough troops to destroy the Saddam regime, their troop strength was insufficient to occupy the country over the long haul. Their strength was such that they could not move Iraq from a state of disorder caused by the war to one of stability.

Almost from the very beginning of the war, opposition to the 'occupation' by paramilitary forces emerged.[41] At first, the insurgency was not well organized. The attacks were mainly aimed at American forces, the favoured weapon used against them being the improvised explosive device (IED). Before long, it was clear that the Americans especially, but also their British allies, were involved in a guerrilla war. By the end of 2003, American military deaths totalled 500.[42]

Already in 2003, but increasingly in 2004, insurgents also began to target the US-supported Iraqi government. Officials, police and military recruits, and strong supporters of the government were all attacked. So also were government buildings and facilities (e.g. power stations, oil pipe-lines and pumping stations). Now the emphasis was more on employing terror tactics than fighting a classic guerrilla war. After viewing the dismembered bodies of their comrades, many police recruits were terrorized into leaving their posts. Power-station workers quit their jobs when they viewed the bomb damage to their station. And ordinary citizens stayed home and expressed less confidence in their government after bombs began to explode in market-places, shopping centres, mosques and just about everywhere. Those who could, began to leave the country.

By 2005 it was clear that all the explosions, killings and kidnappings had taken a new turn. It was no longer enough to attack the 'occupiers' and the government officials who supported them. There was evidence that some of the targeting was sectarian. Sunnis began to attack Shias, and Shias began to attack Sunnis. — *civil war*

The level of sectarian violence was gradually spiralling from bad to worse, but was not quite out of control. However, an event in February of the next year provided the drama to plunge the country into chaos. *2006* The event was the destruction of the famous Golden Dome Mosque in Sammara.[43] Allegedly, the attack was made by Sunni insurgents, although some claim that al-Qaeda was responsible. Whatever the case, the Sunnis were blamed. Shiite responses, inflamed ones, were inevitable. So were responses to those responses. Each act by one side demanded revenge from the other. Seemingly there was no way to end the cycle of vengeance.

Mixed into this unholy revenge struggle were criminals who pretended to be rebels aiming to liberate their country from the Americans, the British and a corrupt Iraqi government. Worse still was a developing struggle even among the Shia groups, each attempting to position itself to be a powerful player in whatever government emerged once some stability returned to Iraq.

So now, in addition to attacking the 'occupiers' and the occupier-sponsored government, various insurgent groups became involved in an interreligious struggle. As Sunnis and Shiites savaged each other, it became increasingly difficult to know how to characterize what was going on. Was it a civil war? A guerrilla war? Or simply a series of chaotic attacks and counter-attacks by various militia forces? However described, it was clear that terrorism was flourishing. When Sunnis attacked Shiites in those neighbourhoods where the Sunnis are in the majority, the Shiites were often terrorized into leaving. Conversely, Shias terrorized Sunnis into leaving parts of Iraq where they were the dominant force.

In 2007 the situation deteriorated still further. All the insurgent groups involved in the struggle learned to make or acquired (from Iran?) more powerful and sophisticated weapons.[44] Further, the bombings, both of the martyr and the non-martyr variety, increased dramatically. The total of suicide bombings, for the whole war, was greater than the total for all the wars and struggles past and present. By 2007 the war had generated over a thousand such bombings. Not only had suicide bombings become a daily event but American casualties had risen to well over 3,500. Civilian casualties were also on the increase. It was a rare day in 2007 to hear that fewer than 30 civilians had been killed. As to the insurgents, it is estimated that their numbers had increased from about 3,000 in 2003 to some 20,000 in 2006.[45] It was difficult by 2007 to find any good news from the Iraq front, unless one was a member or supporter of the insurgency. Matters had so deteriorated that President Bush decided to send over 30,000 extra troops to help contain the violence, especially in Baghdad. As of this writing, it remains to be seen what effect, if any, this increase in troop structure will have on the plight of the Iraqi nation.

5 Political and Military Causes of Terrorism

As our case-studies show, terrorism is not a single monster but a family of such creatures. Acts of terrorism can be state-generated at one extreme, or perpetrated by small, informal, newly formed groups at the other. Terrorists can target innocents exclusively, or attack military and police groups as well as innocents. Further, they can use a wide variety of weapons, including bombs, rocket-propelled grenades, missiles, shells, rifles, chemical weapons, knives and even, as happened in 9/11, civilian airliners. At times, no weapon needs to be used other than the power of the word. Terrorism can terrorize by employing the language of threat. Then there is escape terrorism and martyr terrorism. Terrorism can even vary as to purity. At times it can be used exclusively as a tactic; at other times it is employed in conjunction with other military tactics.

It is likely that, given all this variety, the causes of terrorism are going to be varied as well. No single causal account is likely to be satisfactory. However, if we group some terrorist acts or campaigns into three major categories, it is possible to present an account that has some order to it. The first category encompasses state terrorism against other states; the second, state terrorism against internal enemies of the state; the third, non-state terrorism against enemy states. We will start with the first of these categories.

State-versus-state terrorism

State-versus-state terrorism is sometimes caused by technology rather than political considerations. Given the level of technology available to a nation at a certain time and in a certain war, it is as if technology forces that nation to employ terrorism as a tactic of war. The classic case of such military necessity is the RAF bombing campaign against Germany in the Second World War (see case-study in Chapter 3). For the British, the military situation after the fall of France was desperate. Once Barbarossa started the following year (1941), the USSR was in desperate straits as well. Something had to be done to alleviate the situation. The only option available seemed to be to instigate a bombing campaign against Germany. Such a campaign would not only damage Germany in many ways, but also draw fighter planes, anti-aircraft guns and radar equipment away from the eastern front. But, as it turned out, the only way to implement that campaign was through night bombing. Bombing during daylight hours was far more dangerous. British air losses in daylight bombings were such that if such bombings continued, the whole British air fleet would have been destroyed in short order.[1]

Given the weapons it had in hand (1941–45), it seems that Britain had little choice but to use its air fleet in a terrorist campaign against Germany. In theory the British could have modified their air force structure to other purposes (e.g. to fight U-boats), but this would have been costly in terms of time and money, and also may not have been an efficient use of limited military resources.

What we are offering here is a *causal* account of terrorism. Such an account is not to be confused with a *moral-justification* account. It may be that the British were not justified in bombing Germany as they did – especially in 1945. But causally speaking, we can understand why they engaged in terrorism. They did so because their bombers, bombs and bomb-sights were, relatively speaking, not very sophisticated.

Although that is a very large part of the story, it is not the whole of

it. Other military and/or political considerations were at play at the
time. One was the theory developed by some military leaders that
"strategic bombing" represented a new way of fighting that could
avoid a repeat of the costly trench warfare of the First World War. Part
of the theory told its advocates that strategic bombing would impact
future wars decisively. Wars of the future would be quick and, in the
long-run, less costly. That theory was championed by, among others,
Major-General Hugh Trenchard, who for many years was the Chief of
the Air Staff in Britain.[2] Trenchard and others believed that strategic
bombers could successfully penetrate enemy skies in daylight and
then deliver bombs on enemy key military and industrial targets with
some accuracy. Of course, prior to the war the theory was untested. It
wasn't until well into the Second World War that the RAF realized
that its untested theory was flawed. Still, the theory played a role in
leading the British down the road to terrorizing the German
population. Prior to reality setting in, the British had made a
commitment to build bombers, purchase facilities, equipment and
bombs to support these bombers, and train personnel to operate
them. In that sense, the theory acted as a causal force on the
terrorism that followed.

   Two other causal forces need to be mentioned. They are closely
related, but have nothing to do with technology. The first concerns
the German bombing campaign during the Battle of Britain. Once
the Luftwaffe started bombing London, Coventry and other British
cities, the British felt that revenge was in order. The second causal
factor concerns the war's brutality in general. The Second World War
had quickly turned into a truly brutal affair. Once the RAF bombing
campaign got underway, it was not unusual for the British to lose
over 300 bombers in one month;[3] and it was also not unusual for
thousands to be killed in one bombing raid. Thousands were killed
on the eastern front in Russia every day as well. Casualties all around
were so high that the numbers began to lose their meaning. Political
and military leaders and their followers became callous toward
death and suffering. That callousness made it easier for bomber

command to order more raids and generate yet more death and destruction.

The technological and other factors that encouraged the RAF to slide into a terrorist bombing campaign did their work on the Americans as well. They had become callous in the process of bombing Germany, even though they had made a greater effort than the British to bomb military targets. It was thus easy for them to transfer this callousness to the Japanese. As with the British, there was a revenge motive present also. However, it was not especially revenge for Japanese bombing practices, but for atrocities committed against American, Philippino, Australian and other prisoners, for the peculiarly savage way the Japanese fought their battles on land, and for Pearl Harbor.

Also, like the British, the Americans brought with them a theory about strategic bombing that tended to raise expectations as to what that way of fighting could accomplish. They did have a new bomber for striking Japan. The B-29, or Superfortress, was bigger, faster, could fly higher and carry a heavier payload than the B-17. But essentially it was the same basic technology used earlier in the war. Bombers still had to fly over their targets to drop their bombs, and the bombs they dropped were still 'dumb'. Throughout the Second World War air power had developed rapidly, but still it had far to go before it could strike with precision. Not surprisingly, then, the Americans, like the British, eventually found that it was safer to strike at night. So they too would find it difficult to hit small and even medium-sized targets at night. Even with their more sophisticated technology, they too were 'forced' to engage in terror bombing.

State terrorism within the state

The causes of state terrorism within the state are quite different from those usually found between one state and another. A case in point is what happened within the Ottoman empire in 1914. The empire entered the First World War on 14 November. It formally sided with Germany and Austria-Hungary, and found itself at war with Britain, France, Russia, Serbia and Montenegro.[4] However, by the beginning of the Great War, the Ottoman empire had been weakened. For all practical purposes, its power resided in what we now know as Turkey. By the war's beginning, the empire had little influence in its outer regions such as in Africa, the Middle East and south-eastern Europe. Yet within Turkey itself there were signs of revival (even before the war started). After a period of government instability, the so-called Young Turks, a largely military group, gained control. Their agenda was focused on the doctrine of pan-Turkism. That doctrine led them to look outside of the fading empire to bring Turkish people together under one flag. It was natural, then, for the Young Turks to look in the direction of the Caucasus. That land was controlled by the enemy, Russia, and was heavily populated by people of Turkish origin. Unfortunately, it was also populated by other people, including the Armenians.

The Armenians are an independent-minded Christian people. Back in 1914 they would have preferred (as they no doubt still do) to control their own destiny. It did not please them to live under Russian rule or, as some of them did, under Ottoman rule. Understandably, their loyalties vacillated so as to correspond with what they perceived were their own interests. The Turks saw them as unreliable in their dealings with the Russians. Some Armenians, in fact, turned away from the Ottoman empire/Turkish state to fight with the tsar's army. The Turks did not take kindly to this 'turncoat' behaviour. Furthermore, they feared that the Armenians would sponsor a rebellion (with Russian encouragement) to the rear of their lines as they faced the Russians. To deal with the situation, the Turkish government ordered the execution of some Armenian leaders, deported others and then, later, decided to deport (during 1915–17) the general population of Armenians who lived at or near the front facing the Russians.[5]

The deportation process was both cruel and ill-organized.[6] There were massacres in scores (some say hundreds) of villages. Rape and looting were common. The terrorized Armenians moved away from their homes as they were told to do, but did so under horrible conditions. Food and shelter were in short supply as they headed toward Syria and Mosul in what is now Iraq. The result was that perhaps over a million Armenians died from cold, lack of food, disease and gun-shot wounds.

What happened to the Armenians was not a case of pure terrorism. The Turks simply wanted to get rid of many Armenians so they could have a purer Turkish state – one not corrupted by Christians. So many Armenians were simply deported. But many others were killed or deported, so as to terrorize others into moving away from Turkey.

What were the causes of these horrible events and, in particular, what were the causes of the terrorism against the Armenians? They come down to three. The first is the doctrine of pan-Turkism. This doctrine drove the Turks to do whatever they could to create a Turkish state that would bring as many of the Turks scattered in the region into the fold as possible. If that meant stepping on the toes of other groups, then that was just too bad. Second, and correspondingly, there was a lack of concern for ethical issues. It is as if pan-Turkism consumed all the concerns the Turks had and so left no space for concerns having to do with others and so with ethics. The third cause is discounting. Because the Armenians were perceived as threatening the pan-Turkism cause and because, after all, they were not followers of Islam, it was relatively easy for the Turks to discount Armenian humanity. Thus, killing, maiming or abusing Armenians were not viewed as activities that were immoral in any real sense of the word.

In sum, it was as if the range of Turkish ethical concern included Turks but excluded the Armenians and everyone else. Given that kind of thinking, it is understandable that the Turks lapsed into policies that led to deporting the Armenian population and led as well to the adoption of policies that included terrorism.

— Ethnic Cleansing.

The terrorism found within Germany starting in the 1930s had much in common with that found within Turkey. The targets now were mainly the Jews living in Germany, Austria and Czechoslovakia. As in Turkey, the goal, at least initially, was to deport an unwanted people. To that end, the Nazis resorted to violence early on. Storm troops (SA) and defence corps personnel (SS) arrested Jews in their homes, offices and shops.[7] They then tortured those arrested before releasing them. Upon hearing and seeing what had happened to those arrested, the effect on many was to take steps to leave Germany as soon as possible. But the German government did not restrict itself to these paradigmatic terrorist means in order to get the Jews out of Germany. Using its legal powers, the German government passed laws throughout the 1930s making life in Germany wretched for the Jews. Laws were passed to exclude Jews 'from such occupations as assessors, jurors, and commercial judges'.[8] Other laws were passed banning Jews from working in the entertainment business, for the press and even on farms. Later in the 1930s laws were passed depriving Jews from owning property, forbidding Jewish doctors from treating 'Aryans', and mandating that all Jewish passports be marked with the letter 'J'.[9] To be sure, these legal actions do not completely follow the paradigm scheme of terrorism as identified in Chapter 1. That paradigm tells us that the victims of terrorism are usually a select few. They are harmed and that harm terrorizes others so that they act in ways that please the terrorists. However, with many of these laws, whole segments of the Jewish population and in some cases all of it, were affected. They were all victimized and presumably all (except those who were executed) were terrorized. Still, it seems appropriate to treat the legal manoeuvres of the Nazi regime as an aspect of a terrorist campaign. The laws, affecting almost everyone, had the same effect as did the violence in the 1930s that victimized a few. In both cases, there were victims (a few or many), and the effect on the victims was to frighten the victims themselves and others into leaving Germany.

The campaign of terror was successful. Hundreds of thousands of

Jews left Germany, Austria and Czechoslovakia before the war started. Once it started, still more left if they were able to. But as the war spread and Germany occupied more lands such as Poland, Norway, the NetherLands, France, Yugoslavia, Greece and finally the western parts of the USSR, more Jews came into the Nazi orbit. Also, as the war spread, it became more difficult to find a place for the Jews outside of Greater Germany. The Nazis began killing Jews, and others, in increasingly large numbers as a way of getting these unwanted people out of their domain. It is said that over a million were shot within the occupied lands of the USSR. But shooting was too public, repugnant to many German soldiers and too slow. A more efficient way had to be found. The essence of the Final Solution was, of course, the gas chambers.

As the Nazis moved to solve their Jewish problem, they were less involved in terrorism. This sounds paradoxical. One would suppose that as the killings increased so would the terrorism. However, once the Nazis got their Final Solution organized, they were in a position to employ other means to accomplish their ends. They used sheer military and police power to move their victims to the concentration camps. They also used deception so that those who were moved away from the ghettos, villages, farms, etc. were made to cooperate. Terror certainly was still present because of the rough treatment many received during the process. But late in the war terror became a secondary means for the Nazis. Their primary means for getting the results they wanted was simply the elimination of the undesirables.

Unlike what happened in Turkey in 1914, what happened in Germany when the Nazis took over was not caused by a present and serious threat. The Jews and the others who were victimized by the Nazis were people doing their best to live their lives as best they could in a country that would not fully accept them. And that begins to explain the terror and the killings that followed. All these people were sometimes tolerated, but at other times not. There were always incidents of intolerance to go with the periods of tolerance. The intolerance was there long before the First World War. But these incidents became more common because of the defeat that Germany suffered in that war, and the serious economic situation that followed. Blame had to be assigned to someone for these unfortunate events, and the Jews looked like good candidates for this assignment.

Still, something more has to be said about the causes of the terrorism within Germany and its occupied lands. Something had to happen to set a spark that led to the various holocausts of the Second World War. What happened was the emergence of the Nazi party and its leader Adolf Hitler. Even before, but especially after they came into power, the Nazis effectively dramatized their anti-Semitic and, more generally, their racist views. They effectively supplemented their propaganda campaign with violent acts against Jews and other groups. These acts were either cheered or viewed with casual indifference by the general population. From there, as the Nazis gained complete control of the German government, it was a small step to the creation of their killing machines.

In one sense, the causes of terrorism and other forms of violence in Turkey and Germany are similar. Both felt the need to deport those who were unwanted in the homeland. Both justified their deportation practices by constructing an ideology. In the case of the Turks that ideology was pan-Turkism. The unfortunate Armenians happened to get in the way of that ideology and as a result were smashed. Germany too, controlled after 1933 by the Nazis, had an overarching ideology that could be called pan-Germanism. The Germans needed living space, and they were willing to destroy anyone or group that got in the way of their greater-Germany programme. But unlike the Turks, they also had in their midst a hated minority. It was a powerful minority that had caused Germany pain in the past. The Jews, then, were not just in the way. The trouble they had (allegedly) caused placed them in a position to represent an important part of the German (Nazi) ideology. Given their way of thinking, it was probably easier for the Germans to take steps to destroy the Jews than it was for the Turks to destroy the Armenians.

Non-state terrorism

Some forms of non-state terrorism have already been discussed in earlier chapters. It should be evident already that their causes differ considerably from those of either internal or external state terrorism. State terrorism seems to be mostly caused by threats, real or imagined, to the state. Non-state terrorism seems mostly caused by occupation. At least that is the thesis of Robert Pape. Pape focuses his analysis primarily on martyr terrorism rather than on all forms of the phenomenon. What he says is that martyr terrorism emerges as a way of encouraging (making?) the enemy who occupies one's country to leave. For him, 'Suicide terrorism is an extreme strategy for national liberation.'[10] He cites as evidence of his causal account, the following struggles:[11]

1. Lebanese Shia (Hezbollah presumably) vs US/France/Israel (in the 1980s)
2. Tamils vs Sri Lanka (ongoing)
3. Palestinians vs Israel (ongoing)
4. Sikhs vs India
5. Kashmiris vs India
6. Chechens vs Russia (ongoing)
7. Iraqi rebels vs United States (and also Great Britain: ongoing)

Presumably one could add Afghanistan to the list, since the Taliban seems intent on making a comeback against an occupation and since they too seem to have learned the art of martyr terrorism.

Pape realizes that occupation alone cannot explain martyr terrorism. After all, occupation presumably helps to trigger forms of terrorism where martyrdom is not an issue. So he is forced to look for at least one other factor to explain how the majority of ordinary forms of terrorism graduate to martyr terrorism. The factor he points to the most is religious difference. If the occupier belongs to one religion, and those being occupied belong to another, the chances increase that cases of martyr terrorism will appear. Pape adds one other factor into the mix. He argues that martyr terrorism will normally appear when the occupier has a democratic form of government.[12] More than autocratic governments, it is supposed by the terrorists that democratic governments are less willing to suffer the high number of casualties associated with martyr terrorism.

But a more general causal account of non-state terrorism can be generated by adapting Pape's account of martyr terrorism. It would go something like this.

Many members of a group living in a nation are upset because they are suffering from occupation. Either a foreign power or the dominant ethnic group within a nation is the occupier. More often than not, it is not just a matter of occupation, but also of exploitation.[13] Once the victim group realizes that its victim status is permanent it will begin to rebel. It will do so under the banner of righteousness. The rebels will claim that they are fighting in accordance with moral standards, and fighting against an enemy that lacks such standards.

In the beginning, the rebellion might be in the form of a series of disconnected guerrilla attacks. Because, at the beginning, it has no central command structure, the rebellion will target not just 'enemy' military facilities and personnel, but civilians cooperating with the enemy as well. Ordinary civilians might be also attacked. Different groups within the rebellion will have different agendas.

Early on in the rebellion, it may be difficult to label what is happening as a guerrilla or a terrorist struggle. The two kinds of struggle often fuse. After the rebellion is well under way, the terrorist component of the struggle usually becomes clearer. Partly this greater clarity emerges because of how the attackers label their activities. Using the mass media they tell the world what they are doing. But even if they do not speak up, their intent becomes clearer as they fall into an attack-pattern. Clarity now is in the eyes of the victims. They know first-hand what is going on.

There is at least one other aspect to the process. Usually, but not always, it represents an additional step. If that campaign is flagging, the terrorists will understandably wonder what they can do to reinvigorate it. They can simply up the ante quantitatively. Instead of initiating ten bombings each month, they can move to 20 or 30. But they can also sponsor a qualitative leap in their campaign. They can begin engaging in martyr terrorism. The reason they might do this is that they know, or think they know, that this form of terrorism is more effective than escape terrorism. It is, they believe, harder to stop, easier to carry out, and more frightening to the target population. Terrorists are not blind. They see via the mass media and private communications how other terrorists succeed and fail.[14] They then tailor their campaign with a martyr attack here and an escape attack there.

If these conjectures are not too far off the mark, they suggest that the various forms of non-state terrorism have similar causes. It is not as if martyr terrorism is caused by occupation and by religious differences, but other forms of non-state terrorism have their own special causes. Rather, all forms of non-state terrorism are caused by the conditions Pape identifies as belonging to martyr terrorism. The differences that lead some groups to martyr terrorism are marginal. They have to do mainly with the desperate nature of their cause.

These conjectures suggest that it is a mistake to separate ordinary (escape) terrorism from martyr terrorism too much. In theory, to continue these conjectures, it is possible to begin a state vs non-state terror campaign by engaging in martyr attacks. But, more than likely ordinary terror attacks will precede the martyr attacks. Another possibility is that the two kinds of attacks both occur together. Whatever the case, these speculations encourage us to view martyr attacks as one tactic in a struggle among many. There is nothing particularly special about these attacks except perhaps they are more spectacular and no doubt more effective than other forms of terrorist attacks.

So, state vs non-state terrorism is caused by occupation, exploitation and religious differences. That is a large part of the story, but not all of it. The other part returns us to issues of technology. Just as in the Second World War when the world powers 'needed' to adopt terrorist techniques to help win their wars, so non-state groups are pressured to do what they do because of the weapons available to them. As noted earlier in this chapter, these are

RPGs

highly portable weapons such as rifles, light machine guns, small (but often powerful) bombs, rocket-propelled grenades and the like. In a limited way, these weapons can be used against military and even more so against police personnel, but they are ideal for terrorizing and harming a civilian population. So the weapons available to terrorists, insurgents, guerrillas, however one wishes to characterize them, act as secondary causes of their terrorist ways. To be clear, the weapons available to them do not force them to become terrorists, but these weapons surely make it tempting.

One other causal factor should be mentioned. It has to do with the ill-organized nature of many non-nation insurgent and/or rebel groups. Even if such groups are well organized, they can engage in terrorism as the direct result of commands issued by the group leaders. But more often than not, rebel groups are loosely organized at best and no one leader completely controls how they behave. It is almost inevitable, then, that one of these groups will be more radical than the others, and it will choose terrorism or even martyr terrorism as its favourite tactic. It is easy, then, to see how terrorism can get going. Once one of the radical rebel cells tries it and once it succeeds, others will play 'follow-the-leader'.

6 Personal Profiles

Mindset of non-state terrorists

To a large extent, the personal profiles of those who become terrorists are shaped directly by social factors such as those discussed in the previous chapter. If the terrorist campaign is driven by religious persecution, the individual terrorists will be motivated to act to overcome that persecution. If the campaign is mainly ethnic or racial in nature, the individual terrorists will be moved to act to stop or start ethnic cleansing plaguing their people. Combinations are possible, even likely, here. The ethnic identity the terrorists are defending is often inseparably bound up with religion, so they will be fighting to protect both their ethnic identity and their religion.

But these social factors do not just mark out terrorists. Rebels who do not engage in terrorism or do so only occasionally are also influenced. So too are rebel and terrorist supporters, young and old. The influence comes from all directions. It comes from graffiti, the preaching of religious leaders, political speeches, television, radio, newspapers, peer group conversations and school. The following passage taken from Oliver and Steinberg's *Road to Martyrs' Square* is, as they say, a snapshot of how social influences reach down to children who are just starting school, in this case, in Gaza. The passage describes how teachers are intimidated by well-armed young men into grading their students by 'revolutionary criteria'.

Even kindergartners are not exempt from the fervor. Along with the usual nursery rhymes, they are taught songs and chants like this one, which was performed for us in a school in Khan Yunis, with the teacher directing.

> My father brought me a present
> A gun and machine gun
> When I grow up, I will join the Liberation Army
> The Liberation Army told me how to defend my homeland
> Victory, victory over America and Israel!

The teacher stands at the head of the class. 'What is the name of our country?' she asks. 'Palestine!' the children reply in unison. 'Who is the enemy who stole our country?' she asks. 'The Jews!' exclaim the children. 'What shall we do to them?' she asks. 'Strike them with stones!' the children scream.[1]

For some, no doubt, these sociocultural considerations are enough to turn them into terrorists. Why some are so affected while others are not, is a subject for speculation. But those who are affected have usually come under the influence of teachers or tutors who have guided them in the 'right' direction. Others turn to terrorism for personal reasons as well as for sociocultural reasons. Most famous is the case of the young and beautiful Dhanu. She, as we noted earlier (see Chapter 4), was a Tamil Tiger bent on revenge. It was alleged that her brothers had been killed by Indian troops and that she had been gang-raped by them.[2] There is some doubt whether she herself or her mother had been raped.[3] Still, there is ample evidence that she was motivated to kill Ghandi, the former and possibly future Indian leader, for personal reasons. And, no doubt, others have found themselves similarly motivated. The enemy's killing or harming of a parent, child, uncle, friend or even a member of the community is a common enough phenomenon to trigger violent responses in almost any insurrection. The response to the 'enemy's' violence is likely to generate a counter response of 'blood for blood'.[4]

Louise Richardson expresses the following thoughts about revenge that shows how powerful that motive is for terrorists. Speaking of the Chechen 'Black Widows' (see Chapter 4) she says:

The final videotapes made by living martyrs speak incessantly of the desire to avenge the atrocities committed against their communities. Posters and commemorative cards to the martyrs declare, 'The Right of Revenge is Ours'. In the mid-1990s in Gaza, there emerged a popular music genre known as 'revenge songs'. Sometimes the desire is to avenge a personal injury, the death or arrest of a relative, and sometimes it is to avenge the ill-treatment of people they do not know but with whom they identify. Often it is to avenge a sense of humiliation. The longer a conflict continues, the more atrocities there are to be avenged.[5]

ok—but does not justify random violence

Other motives come into play to help explain why individuals become terrorists. By joining a terrorist group, some gain the respect of their peers. Others join to gain self-respect, fame or a happy afterlife. But lest an over-idealized portrait of terrorism should take shape and dominate our thinking, we need to be reminded that some become terrorists for the most selfish of reasons. We noted in Chapter 3 how several of the early Russian terrorists were criminals. Today, in Darfur, many Janjaweed find looting profitable (see Chapter 4); and in Iraq some insurgents are paid well to do their masters' terrorist work. Compared to being unemployed, the offer of pay to get the Americans and British out of Iraq sounds like an offer that many cannot refuse. Kidnapping can also be profitable. Money and wealth come to terrorists in other ways. The Tamils fund their programme by drug-dealing. And, of course, somebody in the terrorist camp has to handle the drugs and the money that comes into terrorist coffers. It is hard to believe that many of these drugs (and much of the money) do not get siphoned off for personal gain. Up and down the terrorist hierarchy, high-minded motives inevitably become sullied by low-minded ones.

An account of what leads individuals to become terrorists often moves away from talk about motives to talk about irrationality. Terrorists, it is said, are irrational or crazy. Viewed from the point of view of their victims, the actions of terrorists do indeed seem to be beyond comprehension. What terrorists do seems so cruel and so random that there is no discernable pattern to their actions. It is then assumed that if the terrorists' actions are irrational, the perpetrators of these actions must also be irrational. It does not occur to those who make such assessments that the problem lies with them. They just may not have tried hard enough to find a pattern that makes sense of terrorist behaviour.

But even if one tries hard to understand the psychology of terrorists, one may still believe that they are just plain crazy, and that insanity must play an important role in triggering a good deal of terrorism. What terrorists do, the argument continues, cannot but help to attract a certain number of those who are mentally unstable. Richardson responds to such an argument as follows: 'But terrorists … are, by and large, not crazy at all. Interviews with current and former terrorists as well as imprisoned terrorists confirm that the one shared characteristic of terrorists is their normalcy, insofar as we understand the term.'6

It is not quite clear what Richardson is saying here. She is telling us that most terrorists are sane. That is clear, and no doubt true. But the expression 'by and large' leaves the door open for insanity. One can only speculate here, but there must be a certain minority of mentally unstable individuals who are attracted to terrorism and, very likely, a certain number of sane individuals who become unstable after they work at the brutal business of killing people on a regular basis. As we saw in Chapter 3 with the early Russian revolutionaries, insanity among terrorists is not unknown. It is likely, then, insanity plays a significant role in explaining why terrorists become terrorists. Lacking any sound evidence about the matter we can at least speculate that some terrorists are not fully sane. (We will return to this subject later.)

The present account explains why terrorists join the club only in terms of the narrow versions of terrorism identified in Chapter 1. In that chapter, one narrow version restricts terrorism to attacking innocents (civilians, etc.). Another restricts terrorism in terms of who can be a terrorist. Richardson holds to this second restrictive sense. She says that 'terrorism is the act of sub-state groups, not states.'7 The account of personal terrorist motivation given in this chapter so far fits her narrow definition of terrorism as being sub-state in nature. However, in the present work we are also dealing with terrorism in the broad sense that includes state actors. Thus we need to ask the following question. How is the motivation of those conducting terrorist actions on behalf of the state different from or the same as that of sub-state actors?

Mindset of state terrorists

The answer seems obvious. There are differences. Most state actors do not join the military in order to engage in terrorist activities. They sign up or are drafted to do the military work assigned to them, whatever that might be. Those flying in Lancaster bombers in the British Royal Air Force during the Second World War probably had no idea what they would be asked to do before the bombing campaign against Germany got seriously underway. Nor did American B-29 bomber personnel know that they would become terrorists over the Tokyo sky when they first signed up to fight the Japanese and Germans. They didn't know what they would become until their general, Curtis LeMay, told them that they would come in low over Tokyo and then drop fire bombs on a city with many wooden buildings and full of civilians. Even then, many did not realize the extent of their terrorist acts. When bombing at several thousand feet in the dark, it is easy to think of the enemy merely as a target, and even to imagine that the damage done is mainly to military installations.

In contrast, non-state actors cannot so easily fool themselves as to what they are doing. They join up to be terrorists, plan as terrorists do, and then execute their terrorist plan knowing full well what they are up to. These differences between state and non-state terrorists help to explain why we hesitate to append the label of terrorist to many state terrorists. We realize that these state terrorists don't necessarily concentrate on doing terrorist work. Non-state terrorists, real terrorists we are tempted to say, do nothing but that kind of work. They are full-time terrorists.

So there is a big difference between the psychology of non-state and state terrorists at least when we focus on terrorists who do their damage from the sky. However, when we move down to state terrorists operating on the ground, the differences between state and non-state terrorists tend to evaporate. Think here of the Nazi SS organization (Schutzstaffel). The SS had its origins in the mid 1920s.[8] Under the leadership of Heinrich Himmler, it gradually evolved into a powerful organization designed to fight communism. Some came into the SS to help in that fight. Others were taken in by the fervour of the group. There was an air of excitement present among SS members. After all, from the very beginning, it was understood that future leaders would emerge from the SS. It was all very exciting. Still others were evidently attracted to the SS because they were inclined to violence, and it was known that the SS did not discourage that sort of behaviour.[9]

It is true that the early SS members probably did not know to what extent they would be engaged in terrorist violence. Much of that was to come with the invasion of Poland and, eventually, Russia. So in that sense, early SS membership was somewhat like the membership in the RAF. Still, their Nazi ideological fervour tended to make many of them more like non-state terrorists. These SS members believed, as do most non-state terrorists, that the horrible things they did were morally justified. As SS members they were protecting the German government from all sorts of evil. The psychological profile of many SS members thus seems to fall somewhere between those who engaged in terrorism from the air during the Second World War and those who, since then, terrorize for non-state groups.

In another way, the mental state of many SS members differs, on the one side, from those who bombed cities during the Second World War and, on the other, from non-state terrorists. The SS probably had more members who were mentally sick (i.e. were sadists, etc.) than either of these groups. Evidently, the Nazis did very little to screen such people from SS ranks.

Mindset of martyr terrorists

But what of the psychological profiles of suicide terrorists? Are they, at base, like any of the terrorists, state or non-state, characterized so far? Or, in their motivation, are they unique and so are to be characterized psychologically in their own terms?

The story of Dhanu suggests the need for a unique explanatory account. In her culture, rape is a more than a matter of causing physical and mental harm. A raped woman is socially harmed as well. She is shunned socially and, more than likely, cannot marry and thus cannot have (legitimate) children. She becomes a nobody in her society. That being so, one can imagine Dhanu and other women like her thinking that they have nothing more to lose. They might as well end their lives doing something to regain a sense of honour. Their one act of martyrdom takes away their disgrace and turns them into heroines.

In Dhanu-like stories, we have what sounds like a satisfactory explanation as to why some women seek martyrdom. Mia Bloom makes the point that 'In Chechnya, the Black Widows are female suicide bombers who have often lost a loved one. Widowhood may sever the woman from productive society and/or leave her with a sense of hopelessness, especially in traditional societies.'[10] But most suicide terrorists are not associated with dramatic or personally tragic biographies. So the question remains: What drives these individuals to become not just ordinary terrorists but suicide terrorists?

At this point one thinks, once again, of insanity. The supposition is that even if insanity is not a major factor in causing ordinary terrorism, it must be a significant factor in causing martyr terrorism. Richardson disagrees. She claims that research on the subject does not show that insanity is a significant factor in turning individuals into martyr terrorists. She claims that many martyr candidates are carefully selected and then supervised carefully by their mentors, usually in a group of other candidates. Hamas, she reports, claims that it has more volunteers than it can use, so it can afford to be choosy. She makes the same point with respect to the Palestinian Islamic Jihad. A PIJ spokesman is reported as saying 'We do not take depressed people.' She adds: 'Fayez Jaber, speaking for the al-Aqsa Brigades, also insists that his organization accepts only fully mature, psychologically sound volunteers.' The truth, she concludes, is that 'suicide terrorists are not crazy in any meaningful sense of the word'.[11]

The most convincing part of Richardson's argument concerns choice. If it is true that in the struggle against Israel, the various rebel groups have more volunteers for martyr missions than they can use, then there is no need for them to choose those who are severely depressed or seriously mentally sick in some other way. Besides, these people probably are not the most reliable martyr candidates. Their illness may prevent them carrying out their mission. Still, one wonders whether rebel leaders are to be believed when they tell us that they never intentionally use the mentally ill on these missions. In part their denial that they use such people may be a public relations exercise. It would not look right to their general public, and to the locals who tend to supply the martyr candidates, if the mentally sick were exploited by those who administer the various martyr campaigns. Also what martyr spokesmen say may show how they mislead even themselves. Who, one wants to ask, are these people who make these assessments of sanity and insanity? Are they trained psychiatrists or psychologists? Probably not. And even if they are, how can we be certain that they have not chosen martyr candidates who are marginally mentally sick? It is the marginally sick who are still able to function that one wonders most about. And psychiatrists and psychologists are not infallible.

Moreover, those making the decision to pick a martyr candidate have a conflict of interests. Are we to believe that if the martyr managers find a mentally unwell martyr candidate who is nonetheless pliable and reliable they would turn the candidate down?

But there is still some reason to doubt that a good number of suicide terrorists are mentally ill. In Israel and Palestine suicide missions are few and far between. So, as noted already, there is time for those who guide the martyrs to select and train their charges. The same is true in Sri Lanka and many other places where suicide martyrdom is in fashion.

However, in Iraq, and to a lesser extent in Afghanistan, martyrs are created on a daily basis. One cannot help but wonder whether and what kind of screening of the sick from the healthy is possible under the circumstances. Yet even if we can speculate that insanity is more of a factor in Iraq than in other places, and even more of a factor than the 'mentors' of the martyr candidates say it is in Palestine, Sri Lanka and other places, it still may not explain most of the martyrdom found there.

So what might? Certainly if not insanity, the causal factor must have to do with disaffection. The martyr candidates must be frustrated about or angry with some political or social condition. But even disaffection alone cannot explain martyrdom since many others are disaffected and choose instead to escape rather than become martyr terrorists. It could be that martyr-terrorist candidates are more disaffected than the escape candidates. But it is hard to prove such a claim. Political disaffection is not normally measured by degrees. Those disaffected, whether they resort to escape or martyr terrorism, tend to be all disaffected to the extreme. In their eyes, their side is completely right, the other side completely wrong.

As we have noted already, disaffection alone does not explain why individuals become terrorists, let alone martyrs. So, at best, it is a necessary condition for explaining why individuals move in the direction of martyr terrorism. For a more complete explanation, what is needed is a more comprehensive account of what goes on in the minds of martyr candidates well before, just before and just as they make their move to martyrdom. Yes, disaffection is there, but some other mental states must be there as well. What might these states be? What emerges from various accounts put together from interviews of martyr candidates, of those who failed in their attempt to become martyrs, and from those who knew the martyrs, is that there is no single, shared mental state to explain martyrdom.[12] For one candidate, martyrdom is chosen because it seems like the most effective tactic available for harming the enemy. For another, martyrdom is a way of regaining self-respect after being repeatedly humiliated by the enemy. For still another, it is the way of regaining self-respect after being unemployed for a long period of time. For still another, it is religious redemption in the next life. For yet another, it is a way of responding to having been witness to the killing of a child or some other helpless human being. For some, entering the domain of martyrdom is an escape from an unhappy family life. For most, more than one of these mental states are present at the same time. Together, they encourage the potential martyr to approach someone in charge of the martyr campaign and offer his or her body for the cause.

As reported from various interviews, then, the mental states of martyr candidates are extremely varied and complicated. But they may be even more complicated than the interview process suggests. We all have private mental states that we are reluctant to share even with our closest friends, let alone with an interviewer who is recording or writing down everything we say. A terrorist candidate may be suffering from guilt for having failed to help his family when it was in distress. Or the guilt may come from a woman who failed to deliver a male child to her husband. Or if not guilt, the candidate may have a sense of inferiority that she never talks about. Or there might be a strong sense of resentment that the younger son feels toward his older brother. Any one of these subtle feelings can play a role in leading a person to choose martyrdom.

One other caution should be kept in mind in assessing the mental states of those who present themselves as martyrs. The reasons these candidates (and the failed martyrs) give to those who interview them very likely contain normative components. That is, the reasons they give publicly may be coloured to make the candidate look good, or may be what the candidate thinks that interviewer (and viewers) wants to hear. As a result, the very process of gaining information about these candidates may present an idealized portrait of a candidate's mind when, in fact, that mind is host to less than ideal thoughts. However, this caution does not affect our overall point about the mental states of martyr candidates: namely, that these states are extremely complicated and varied.

Once the step is taken, and once the volunteer is accepted by the martyr leaders, the candidate may find that backsliding is almost impossible. In addition to providing training, the martyr mentors parade all the rhetoric of the cause before the candidate.[13] Any tendency to backsliding is thereby checked. Backsliding is also checked by a socializing process. Once the candidates are accepted, they are often placed in 'martyrdom cells'.[14] These cells, of three to five candidates, are made up of individuals from the same extended family or community. Inevitably a strong sense of solidarity develops within the cell. Now, if backsliding again surfaces, it faces the scrutiny of the cell, of the mentoring team and perhaps the volunteer's family and friends. To back out now would be to be shamed.

> In a video called *The Giants*, three soon-to-be martyrs take turns on center stage before coming together to make a collective vow to complete the operation. They had been told that 'In Islam it's a horrible thing to run away' and that there is a verse in the Koran that says that anyone who runs away in the middle of a battle goes straight to Hell.[15]

So we add to the complicated motivation of martyr candidates before they join their mentoring group, the very different motivation these candidates have after they join up. After joining, their beliefs are sharpened and made more intense. And their commitment is firmed up. In the end, then, what we likely have is a young, idealistic and easily impressionable individual putting on a bomb-belt or driving a bomb-laden car or truck to his or her doom. Once it is over, the martyr is celebrated by his family, peers and the community. Knowing that this celebration will take place is also part of what motivated him/her to do what he/she did in the first place. Further, that celebration serves to motivate the next generation of 'volunteers' to add their bodies to the list of those who are known as martyrs.

7 The Future of Terrorism

Persistence

This chapter explores the question of whether terrorism is likely to persist. Many, if not most, writers suppose that terrorism will not go away soon. They give reasons at to why it is likely to persist, but more often than not they do so in piecemeal fashion. In this chapter, the persistence question is dealt with in a more systematic, albeit speculative, way. Only then is it possible to judge whether we are likely to have to live with the phenomenon of terrorism for a long time.

But where to begin? The obvious place is at the level of terrorist motivation. From there, we shall consider the human and material resources that might be available to terrorists to sustain them. After that, we will look at how terrorists are organized and trained, and how they plan their attacks. Last of all, we discuss the implementation of the terrorist attack. Having canvassed the range of activities that make up the terrorist agenda, the chapter closes with a (preliminary) discussion of the response to terrorism. The question now becomes: Can those who are targeted by terrorism respond in such a way as to keep terrorism from becoming persistent?

Motivation

As we have already noted in previous chapters, terrorist motivation is high because of terrorists' sense of their just cause. Most terrorists see themselves as fighting for righteousness. They are keen to liberate their people from those who oppress them militarily, politically and/ or economically. For others, it has less to do with freedom than with taking steps to maintain their group's cultural/religious identity or purity.[1]

"piggy-back" criminals

As we have also noted, there are some engaged in terrorist-like activities who have no noble motives. At present, some of these are pirates operating off various Indonesian islands.[2] They 'piggy-back' on established terrorist movements operating at sea so that, for all appearances, they have the same effect on sea commerce as do genuine terrorists. There are also gangster 'terrorists', as in Iraq, who piggy-back on whatever local insurrection is taking place. But these people represent a minority. They do not seriously detract from the point that most terrorists conceive of themselves as fighting for a noble cause.[3]

It is easy to miss this point if one listens to the rhetoric that commonly follows terrorists. They are not merely called terrorists, the pejorative term of choice these days in international affairs, but are also called mindless, senseless, irrational and evil. All these terms suggest that what terrorists do is incomprehensible. Immersing oneself in this rhetoric, it just makes no sense to suggest that terrorists could possibly play a role in a righteous cause.

But such are the dangers of using the rhetoric of hyperbole. Clearly, what is called for is some rhetorical restraint. Instead of throwing ugly names at terrorists, what is needed is a descriptive account of why terrorists do what they do. That is what we have been doing in all the previous chapters, but most especially in Chapters 5 and 6. Such an account opens up the mind to the possibility that terrorists might just be fighting for a just cause.

If terrorists were coerced or simply paid to fight, they likely would lose heart in the face of serious military challenges. However, motivated as many of them are by a cause, especially by one associated with their religion and/or their national pride, they will not fade away easily. Their rhetoric, coming as it does mainly from their religious and political leaders, cannot help but sustain their cause.

Human and financial resources

But no matter how strong they are, motives can at best represent the necessary conditions in accounting for the persistence of terrorism. Human and other resources are also needed. Are such resources likely to be available in large enough numbers to help trigger and then sustain various terrorist movements?

Surely the terrorists' sense of righteousness is found not just in those who are already in terrorist camps. If the cause that motivates terrorists has some basis in reality, others will get the feeling of righteous indignation and join up. They will get the feeling especially if the terrorists are adept at communicating their message on television and radio, newspapers and the Internet. So personnel recruitment is not likely to be a problem. It is not a problem for another reason. Terrorist groups do not need a large number of recruits the way regular armies do. If need be, they can sustain themselves by recruiting a small handful of replacements. Think here of what is happening in Iraq. About 25,000 insurgents are facing American, British and Iraqi forces that number around 500,000.

Nor is money a problem. The same motives that move terrorists to action will move many who cannot fight to give financial support to the cause. To be sure, for a variety of reasons, things could go badly for the terrorists and so the supply of recruits and financial supporters could dry up. But any number of terrorist movements will probably stay active so long as a modest amount of money comes into their coffers. Terrorist groups don't need to buy expensive military equipment such as fighter planes, helicopters and tanks. All they need is money for rifles, rocket-propelled grenades and bomb-making supplies.

So far, then, in terms of human and other resources, it appears that terrorists can rather easily sustain themselves. And they can do more than that. Their rhetoric and their public actions can inspire the formation of new groups to sustain their cause. In addition, they can inspire new groups in other parts of the world who wish to champion their own causes. These groups will observe how effective terrorism has already been in the defence of other causes. They are likely to respond by saying 'me too'. The model of how to fight for one's cause in the face of strong national political and military forces is in place.

Organization and training

But what of organizational matters? There are times when a central command structure suits the purposes of a terrorist organization. Probably they will be rare. Such a structure facilitates coordination. However, terrorist (and guerrilla) groups have always understood the dangers of centralization. Once their enemies get themselves organized to respond to a terrorist threat, they can destroy a well-organized movement in domino-effect fashion either by attacking the central command structure itself or by neutralizing a few of the dominos. To avoid that effect, the links between the cells of a terrorist organization need to be kept loose. This means that coordination will suffer. The cells now are free to pursue their own agendas, even if this means that they may at times be working at cross-purposes. But this is the price to ensure survival. A loose structure does not suffer from the domino effect when the members of one cell are captured, tortured and/or killed.

A loosely structured organization has another advantage, or perhaps it is better to say that it does not suffer from a disadvantage. Most terrorist operations are not so complicated as to require extensive cooperation (9/11 is the exception rather than the rule). So, individual and independent cells can both do their work and do it in the confines of a loosely linked organization, and survive.

Because most terrorist operations are not hugely complicated, training terrorists poses no special challenges. Indeed, training can be made relatively easy when terrorist cells specialize. Mastering a wide range of military skills is not necessary for any one cell when all it does is bomb roads or engage in martyr bombings. Presumably the specialty operation that a cell chooses is one its founders already know something about. They then pass on their skills to new members in a reasonable period of time. If anything, if it is easy to train new recruits to replace the 'old guard', it is likely that terrorist groups will not only persevere but also flourish.

Terrorism is more likely to persevere for another reason. If training a terrorist to do his work is relatively easy then that represents another reason why new groups can emerge 'out of the blue' rather easily. So together with a loosely structured organization, the ease of training recruits gives terrorism the momentum to keep things going.

Planning

There is a factor related to training that also contributes to the persistence of terrorism: namely, planning. Like any group trained to engage in violence, terrorists plan in secret. But terrorists have an advantage here. Since their groups are small and also difficult to infiltrate, their secrets are less likely to leak out than those of their more powerful but cumbersome enemies. Their real advantage, however, is in planning flexibility. Terrorists can lie low as long as they please and then strike when they please. When lying low they have to be careful. But this period of planning and training is not particularly costly or dangerous to terrorists. It is surely more costly and dangerous for their opponents. The opponents have a choice.

Either they do nothing to get ready for the next attack, and as a result suffer grievously when it comes, or they spend much effort and resources preparing for that attack. In effect, the terrorists gain by planning patience. It is part of their flexible plan that they keep their enemies nervously waiting for the next blow. Their strategy is to wear down the enemy militarily, economically and politically. Time, they know, is on their side. The only mandate they have is to strike when the enemy's fear of them diminishes. Once they strike again, and if it suits their purposes, they can sit back and watch their enemies scurry around in terror and, in the end, waste away.

Execution

Many have written about the vulnerability of those whom terrorists target, and how easy it is for terrorists to execute their plans. Put simply, those who live in an open society are open to attack.[4] Narrow bands of institutions such as military and airport facilities and some government buildings can be, and are, protected. But other institutions, places and things such as automobiles, (school) buses, bridges, chemical plants,[5] commercial buildings, docking facilities, eating establishments, farms, highways, homes, hospitals, libraries, parks, power stations, trains and tracks, schools, ships, shopping centres, stadiums, water-pumping stations and storage areas are all open, many completely so, to attack.

It should be clear that this openness is to a large extent a new phenomenon. To be sure, some of these targets have always been subject to attack. But today, in contrast with the past, modern open societies are more open than before. There are facilities such as nuclear plants, massive chemical plants, equally massive airport facilities, mass media facilities, sky-scrapers and impressively large bridges that sit there inviting attack. With modern transportation, terrorists can manoeuvre around more of them, attack and then escape more easily than before. They also have increasingly powerful

more powerful + portable weapons

and portable weapons. In this regard the future is bright for terrorism. As technologies trickle down from the rich and powerful to the not-so-rich and not-so-powerful, new weapons will act as 'force multipliers' for all kinds of terrorist groups. Finally, terrorists have available to them means of communication (mobile phones, email, the Internet) so they can coordinate their deadly work in a way that was simply not possible before.

All this is good news for the persistence of the terrorist programme. Notice how this good news differs from the good news about motivation, training and organization, which is not really a new phenomenon. Terrorists have always had righteous causes to motivate them. And, as was pointed out already, terrorists (and guerrilla fighters) have long been aware of the advantages of decentralizing their organization. Finally, training terrorists has always been easier and less costly than training regular soldiers who fight in armies. But the ability of terrorists to move free and undetected among the victims of the modern open society they plan to attack, and their ability to attack with powerful weapons, are new.

the new 'terrorism'

But the news is even better for terrorists than so far portrayed. The enemies of terrorism are more vulnerable not just because their bodies and buildings are more vulnerable. They are more vulnerable psychologically as well. In the past, the psychological effects of terrorism were generally local. Those who actually saw the results of a terrorist attack or who heard about it by word of mouth were very likely terrorized. In days of old, the terror associated with acts of terror spread slowly and dissipated rather quickly. But today, with the aid of the mass media, terrorists get free advertising concerning the quality and quantity of their work. People can view the attacks and the results on television over and over again. Using the mass media, terrorists can today create massive psychological ripple effects with their well-advertised acts of terror. It is difficult to imagine a more welcome gift to their cause.[6]

The targets listed in the previous section are all vulnerable. However, terrorists can also target military and government facilities and personnel.[7] Their target choice is wide indeed and so they have great flexibility when it comes to implementing their attacks. Presumably they will choose when, where and what to strike in accordance with their political aims. But their choices will probably involve more than inflicting maximum terror on their enemies. Their political aims may also be to bring about real damage to the enemy in the same way that standard military operations do damage. Furthermore, terrorist attacks often aim to bring about psychological effects that have nothing to do with terror. Instead, their aim may be to inspire the friends and allies of the terrorists at home and abroad. They may want to bring about a feel-good effect among their people and to inspire others to join or support the cause.

Picking a target thus poses a kind of challenge to terrorists. If the terrorists choose to attack military targets they may well gain credit in the eyes of their own people, but they are unlikely to generate a reaction of terror. Disciplined troops don't panic in the same way that civilians do. But in attacking the military, the intention might not be to panic members of that establishment. Rather, it might be to panic the general population. Still, in attacking the military establishment, casualties among the terrorists are likely to be relatively high. So it is understandable that terrorists would choose to attack military targets only when the situation is just right (e.g. during a holiday when security at a base is lax).

It is more likely that terrorists would attack government buildings. Security in these buildings is significant but still breachable. More than likely, these attacks would not be so costly to the terrorists as attacks on military installations. Further, they are likely to cause a significant number of casualties: enough, perhaps, to weaken the government. In addition, these attacks might gain much prestige for them. They would also create a great deal of terror among government employees and the population at large. Overall, these attacks on the institutions of the enemy government look like a good investment for the terrorists.

Other targets include bridges and infrastructure facilities such as water- and power-plants. These are not the easiest targets to hit but, like government buildings, they are very important to the victim nation. So attacking them is a good investment for the terrorists.

Finally, there are civilian targets: vulnerable and easy to attack. Civilian targets may, however, carry a cost for the terrorists in the form of blame they receive for violating the principle of discrimination. It is usually a cost imposed on them by the victim nation and its allies. Unfortunately, most terrorist groups do not admit that they owe anything to anybody in this regard. As we will see more clearly in the next chapter, they argue that most of their victims are not as innocent as is often supposed, and that attacking them is thus not wrong. Or, they argue, war with monster nation-states is indeed desperate in nature and thus they have no choice but to do all they can to win. However they argue, they try to deflect the argument that they bear much guilt for killing civilians. They rarely convince more than a small minority 'abroad' of the justice of their actions, but they often convince most of their allies and friends. With those who really count for the terrorists, then, there really is little or no cost for attacking civilians.

Thus, as far as the terrorists are concerned, they get a 'free ride' ethically in their attacks on civilians (non-combatants, innocents, etc.). This leaves them in position to assess their terrorist acts in terms of their effectiveness. And like their attacks on government facilities and personnel, and their attacks on the enemy's infrastructure, they have on their hands another good investment. Non-combatants are easy to harm and easy to terrorize. They are also relatively safe targets. If the terrorists have an escape option in their plans, they can often and regularly exercise it.

But what if they plan not to use an escape option? That is, what if they plan a martyr terrorist action? Now there is the cost to be paid of losing one (or more) terrorist lives. For the non-religious martyr, the loss is a loss pure and simple. The martyr is here today, gone tomorrow. For the religious martyr who makes a sacrifice for the cause there is the afterlife to enjoy. So martyrdom is not a total loss.

But whatever the costs to the martyr, it is clear that this form of terrorism is, like the other forms, an excellent investment. Martyr terrorism is not only difficult to defend against; it often can do more damage than escape terrorism. This tactic can be so effective that it opens the door once again for attacks against military installations and personnel. An automobile can approach a checkpoint slowly and then suddenly accelerate. If the soldiers at the checkpoint are drunk, sleepy or just careless, the car with explosives can quickly come into their midst. Or a martyr terrorist in a car can swerve out of his/her traffic lane into an army truck full of soldiers. Ramming bomb-loaded cars or trucks into a bridge or building is relatively easy to do. Likewise martyr terrorist attacks on people in buses, shopping centres and restaurants are relatively easy (although maybe not so easy in Israel).

Beyond the factor of ease of implementation, we have seen that martyr attacks have more terror impact than those which offer the terrorist a means of escape. One is naturally more fearful of those which are willing to give their lives for their cause. The impression they leave is that nothing can stop them. The impression is enhanced if the attacks come two or three at a time, and if it becomes obvious that the number of martyr recruits is not finite.

We will now investigate why all these attacks, on military installations, on the infrastructure and on the so-called innocent of a society, constitute more than a good investment for the terrorists. So far the argument has been that these attacks collect victims and create massive amounts of terror. But terror is not the real aim of terrorists. It is the means. It is what terror *produces* that is the real aim. And among other things it produces economic strain. The 9/11 attack cost the United States hundreds of billions of dollars, quite apart from the costs associated with the Twin Towers, the Pentagon and loss of four airliners. All sorts of businesses, especially airlines, suffered as the result of these attacks. The government suffered as well since it had to pay, and is paying, for the extra security it had to purchase.

But there are social and political costs to be accounted for.[8] People's rights are negatively affected, and political power swings one way and then another. All these effects are brought about in exchange for the lives of a small group of martyrs and a few million dollars needed to plan and execute attacks such as 9/11.

The many martyr attacks on Israel have been less overwhelmingly impressive. But they too have taken a toll on the economy and infrastructure. The terrorist policy seems to be 'lose a few martyrs, do a lot of damage'.

So, overall, for modest costs, terrorist attacks yield astonishing results. Terrorists can hardly be discouraged by the results they have achieved so far. They certainly have no reason at this point in time to abandon their efforts. If they practise the virtue of patience, they may (and probably do) believe that time is on their side. They are not the ones who are paying a high economic and psychological price for sustaining their war on a daily basis. They can wait a month, a year, or whatever span of time they choose, before striking again. The longer the terrorists wait the more their enemies bleed. When the bleeding slows, they can send another wave of terror around the world, thereby cause more economic stress and more political chaos. They can wait especially if they hope to collect more powerful weapons in the future to enhance their terror campaign. Sooner or later, their theory is, the victim nation will collapse or be so weakened as in effect to be defeated.

Terrorists around the world might be wrong about all this. In the end, terrorism as a way of waging war or engaging in violent conflict may fizzle out. But in this chapter we are not speaking about who the eventual winner (or non-loser) will be. Rather, we are speculating about whether terrorism will persist in the near and not-so-near future. And the weight of the argument so far is that there are many factors (high motivation, a decentralized organization, the ease of recruiting and training terrorists, patient planning, the extreme vulnerability of terrorist states and the high impact of terror attacks on people today, etc.) all pointing to one conclusion. Terrorism is likely to be with us for a long time.

One other factor deserves mention. It leads to the same depressing conclusion. At least for now, at the beginning of the century, a demonstration effect is at work. Bin Laden and others in the Middle East and Chechnya have demonstrated how effective the tactic of modern terrorism can be, how easy it is to engage in this tactic and, finally, how easy it is to justify terrorism to themselves. The example they have set cannot help but inspire members of their own group to continue the struggle.[9] But their example will also probably inspire new disaffected groups into thinking of terrorism not as a last but as a first resort they should employ. Others have shown them the way to create disorder. Their duty is to follow.

The victim's viewpoint

We shall now look at terrorism from the point of view of its victims. So far, several factors have been identified as working in the direction of helping to sustain terrorism. The winds all seem to be blowing in one direction. But might it not be possible for victim nations to take steps to slow down the momentum of terrorism? (We shall look at this question in more detail in Chapter 10, but we need to address it also at this point in the discussion of the persistence of terrorism.)

Certainly one step a nation can take to respond to a terrorist threat is to call out its military establishment. This is what happened in Afghanistan, where a coalition of nations led by the United States played an offensive military card. Prior to 9/11 al-Qaeda and the Taliban felt safe. Evidently they felt that they were beyond the reach of the US military's long arm. So, feeling safe, they concentrated their forces in relatively large camps. As it turned out, the US military's reach was longer than they thought. Both al-Qaeda and the Taliban had made a serious miscalculation, and they paid the price.

But they learned their lesson. By spreading out their forces in western Pakistan, they became far less vulnerable. They could still suffer defeat, but it is clear that the military option cannot deliver that defeat in the near future. Further, even if they were defeated in their present location, it is not at all clear that they would give up the fight to cleanse Islam of Western influence. They would probably continue their efforts in other countries such as Egypt, Israel/ Palestine and Saudi Arabia. And further still, even if for some reason al-Qaeda becomes extinct, other groups are likely to pick up the mantle in the cause of Islam. It is also likely that losing in Pakistan (and/or Iraq) would be thought of in 'just for now' terms. A policy of 'democracy today, back to Islam tomorrow' is the one the terrorists most probably would adopt.[10]

But what else can be done to slow the terrorist movement? The political card is to democratize the whole region and thereby create a cluster of just societies in the Middle East and elsewhere. Give people a better government and improve their lives, the argument runs, and terrorism would dry up. That is the agenda that the neo-conservatives in the United States present to us.

There are two points about this agenda. First, it is very ambitious. The process of changing non-democratic regimes into democratic ones, even if successful, is likely to take a long time. And even if it does succeed, backsliding can easily take place (think of what may be happening in Russia with the Putin administration).[11] Second, some Islamists will take offence at democratization. They will look at that process as still another attempt by the West to dominate them. They will see it as another crusade. Such perceptions will probably inspire them to engage in yet more terrorist activity. At worst, then, the political card will fail. At best it promises relief in the far future.

Victims of terrorism have one other card they can play: namely, the military/police card. The card would likely be played on a now-here, now-there basis in response to terrorist attacks here and then there. Playing such a card would involve an extension of the security steps already in place at airports throughout the world. So it would have a preventive component to it.

Playing this card in different combinations might be the right thing to do. But even if it succeeds, it too would take a long time to take effect. In the meantime, terrorism presumably would continue – for all the reasons cited already. Thus, looking at the issue of persistence from either the terrorist's or the anti-terrorist's point of view leads to the same conclusion. On the one side, terrorists have the motivation and the means to continue. On the other, their enemies have the means, *at best*, to slow terrorism down or stop it in the long-run. For a variety of reasons, then, we, the victims of terrorism, will have to get used to living with the new world disorder.

8   Arguments in Defence of Terrorism

Jus ad bellum (just cause)

Those who defend terrorism do not always distinguish between *jus ad bellum* and *jus in bello*. Yet it is important to make that distinction since it helps to organize the many arguments that terrorists and their defenders offer to justify their way of fighting. We begin with the *jus ad bellum* arguments.

The most common argument terrorists cite is that they are engaged in a struggle against aggression, and so have just cause on their side. The Palestinians use this argument against the Israeli invaders. Here is Hamas's account of the Palestinian plight in Article 20 of their 'charter'. This article first praises Allah and the people who followed Allah's righteous path in helping one another when there was a need for help. Article 20 calls this the Islamic spirit and says that all followers of Allah should be imbued with that spirit. Then the article says:

> Our enemy pursues the style of collective punishment of usurping people's countries and properties, of pursuing them into their exiles and places of assembly. It has resorted to breaking bones, opening fire on women and children and the old, with or without reason ...[1]

Hezbollah, in its 'Programme' also sees itself as a fighter against aggression:

> We declare openly and loudly that we are an *umma* [a Muslim
> community] that fears God only and is by no means ready to tolerate
> injustice, aggression, and humiliation. America, its Atlanta Pact allies
> [NATO], and the Zionist entity in the holy land of Palestine attacked us and
> continue to do so without respite ... This is why we are, more and more,
> in a state of permanent alert in order to repel aggression and defend our,
> religion, our existence, our dignity.[2]

Not to be left out, Osama Bin Laden also sees himself and those
who fight with him as opposing aggression. They also blame the
corrupt Saudi regime that invites Western crusader armies into the
sacred lands of Islam. Here Bin Laden is speaking in his famous
declaration of war on just about everybody:

> The latest and the greatest of these aggressions [by the Zionist-crusader
> alliance], incurred by the Muslims since the death of the prophet ... is the
> occupation of the Land of the Two Holy Places – the foundation of the
> house is Islam, the place of the revelation, the source of the message, and
> the place of the noble Kaba [the central Islamic holy site], the *qibla* [the
> direction of prayer] of all Muslims – by the armies of the American
> crusaders and their allies.[3]

The Tamils of Sri Lanka are here too. They see the Buddhist
government as gradually, and at times not so gradually, trying to take
over their corner of that land (see Chapter 4).

A variant of this argument focuses on liberation. Again we see the
Palestinians here, now arguing that Land of Israel has to be given
back to those to whom it properly belongs. In the passage below,
Hezbollah is again speaking in the same 'Programme' cited above:
'Our primary assumption in our fight against Israel states that the
Zionist entity has been aggressive from its inception, and built on
lands wrested from their owners, at the expense of the rights of
Muslim people.'[4]

The Provisional Irish Republican Army, the Chechan rebels, the
Basques in Spain and the Kurds in Turkey all argue along the same
lines. They want either to affirm their autonomy for the first time over

lands they have occupied, or to re-establish autonomy lost in the past.

Understandably, the documents cited above are full of hyperbole. They, and similar ones written by other rebel groups, are intended to be inspirational in nature. They are intended to invigorate their authors' allies in support of the cause. Given their purpose, it would be a mistake for those who are not part of the cause to be put off by the hyperbole and, in so doing, miss whatever messages these documents contain. The messages and the hyperbole have to be sorted out.

But the sorting process is not easy since the hyperbole and the message are intertwined. For example, Bin Laden (see above) labels the coalition's presence in Saudi Arabia for the purposes of launching an attack on Iraq in 1991 an aggression and an occupation. But for him this presence is not just ordinary aggression. Rather, it is the greatest of aggressions against Islam. In addition, he neglects to mention that the coalition was invited into Saudi Arabia by that nation's rulers. The Saudis were afraid that Saddam would move into the north-east part of Saudi Arabia, and thus take control of most of that country's oil supply. To count such an invitation an act of aggression is to undermine to the meaning of 'aggression'. Finally, he fails to mention that the attack on Iraq was designed to undo Iraqi aggression against Kuwait.

In the Hamas charter the hyperbole and the message get mixed together in a different way. Now hyperbole is expressed via exaggeration as when the Israelis are accused of 'opening fire on women and children and the old, with or without reason', as if they are doing these things all the time and as a matter of policy. It may be that women, children and the old are killed in the struggle with Hamas and the other Palestinian rebel groups. But if they are killed, Hamas does not tell us that this often happens because the Israelis are targeting insurgents who are hiding among civilians in urban areas.

Putting aside these and similar examples of hyperbole, the

question is: what remains? And the answer is, quite a bit. In the Middle East the most basic claim is that the Israelis became aggressors when they first took the smallest piece of land from the indigenous population and kept it for themselves. There are, no doubt, arguments on both sides as to whose land what is now Israel really is. We don't intend to enter into that (endless) debate. We don't have to. All that is required is to show that the Palestinians are able to present a plausible case that they are victims of aggression. And, indeed, they have such a case. They are aware that many of their people lost their homes as the result of the 1948 war, and subsequent wars, that many became refugees, and that Palestinian blood was and is being shed in that part of the world.

The Palestinians tell follow-on stories. Following each major war that Israel fought against the Arabs, it is claimed that the Israelis adopted what might be called salami-tactics aggression. A small slice of land is taken over here, another there, and the next thing one notes is that a whole portion of the West Bank is full of Jewish settlers.[5] The Israelis may give in at one point by knocking down certain (small) settlements but, at the same time, other settlements are started or expanded.

Bin Laden and his friends say that they too are fighting non-military as well as military aggression. Non-military aggression takes the form of Western countries co-opting Arab regimes so that these regimes do the bidding of the West. In his eyes, what Western countries are practising is indirect rather than direct colonialism. It involves bribing these regimes so that, among other things, the Muslims living in these co-opted nations end up losing their ethnic and religious identities.

Other rebel groups can, and do, tell similar stories. Their enemies are the aggressors, they say, and they themselves the victims. With respect to just cause, then, all of them claim that they are acting in accordance with that principle while their enemies are not.

In assessing these claims, it is easy to be hypnotized, once again, by hyperbole. Also because it is difficult to disregard the terrorism these groups generate, it is difficult to grant that their causes might be just. However, engaging in role-reversal helps to clear one's head. Imagine a clash between Western cultures and the cultures of Islam, but with the former being dominated by the latter. Imagine further that by using their economic, political and military power, the Islamic cultures are 'penetrating' their Western counterparts. Increasingly, Islamic music is heard on London and Chicago radio stations, more and more people are converting to Islam, Western leaders bow to Islamic pressures so that business is conducted so as to favour Islamic interests, from time to time Islamic military forces act against the weaker Western nations, and democratic institutions in the West are gradually undermined in favour of law as understood by a group of clerics. Finally, imagine being a Western citizen living among all these changes.

The question that would certainly come to at least some Western minds is: Are we justified in resisting these changes? The answer is obvious. 'Yes', they would say, 'we are justified. We have just cause on our side because first in this way and then in that way we are being trampled upon.'

If the West would have just cause on its side were it under attack from stronger Islamic nations, then these nations have just cause when they are under similar attacks from stronger Western nations. Notice, if one accepts this argument, what it shows and does not show. It does not show that the rebels, whoever they are, are justified in engaging in terrorism. All it shows is that one of the major principles of just war theory has been satisfied. The others have also to be satisfied before any organization can say it is fully justified in going to war. Still, if the rebel groups wish to engage in terrorism they need to justify going to war but, in addition, to develop arguments that allow them to become not just rebels but terrorists.

Jus ad bellum (other principles)

Some modern terrorists develop additional arguments to show that they are justified in going to war (i.e. satisfying *jus ad bellum* principles beyond just cause). But others do not. There is just too much variation among terrorists who come from different parts of the world to make statements about just war theory applicable to all or almost all of them. There is even variation among factions within one nation or area of the world. Even so, it is probably fair to say that terrorist movements in general give less attention to the other *jus ad bellum* principles than they do to just cause. They are likely to say a few things about the right intention principles: namely, that their intentions are pure (i.e. in accord with just cause) and their enemies' intentions impure. They also are likely to tell us, more by way of wishful thinking than anything else, that they have a high likelihood of success, and that the good of their revolution far outweighs the bad. They may even say that they are the (self-appointed) legitimate authority for the people they represent. But the discussion of these principles tends to be rather light and sketchy.

One *jus ad bellum* principle that tends to get more attention is last resort. Many terrorists tend to claim that other means before violence have been tried. Usually those trying these means are not the rebels themselves. Other less radical groups have tried negotiations (e.g. in Kosovo, Sri Lanka, Palestine) and have failed. Not only that, so the argument goes, but the enemy has often already resorted to violence prior to negotiation. About such matters, listen, once again, to what Hamas has to say in Article 13 of its charter:

> [Peace] initiatives, the so-called peaceful solutions, and the international conferences to resolve the Palestinian problem are all contrary to the beliefs of Hamas ... Those conferences are no more than a means to appoint the nonbelievers as arbitrators in the lands of Islam. Since when did the unbelievers do justice to the believers? ... There is no solution to the Palestinian problem except by *jihad*. The initiatives, proposal, and international conferences are but a waste of time, an exercise in futility.[6]

What is one to make of such a passage? It sounds like an outright rejection of the last-resort principle? Resorts other than jihad are rejected out of hand. But what Hamas says must be put in the context of their overall thinking. As stated in their charter, their goal is the complete elimination of the present state of Israel. This is a state (they argue) that has come into existence by massive aggression. Lands belonging to Islamic people were taken over by the Jews. Given this view, what resorts short of jihad are there for Hamas? Boycotts? Certainly Hamas can urge Palestinians to implement a business boycott of Israel, but it will be to little effect. Sanctions? Hardly, since Hamas is too weak an entity to apply sanctions to a regionally powerful state. Hamas is too weak even to appeal to other nations to bring sanctions to bear upon Israel. Negotiations? What is there to negotiate? Are the Jews going to enter negotiations whose end-product will be the elimination of Israel? That is ridiculous, and Hamas knows it is. There is, then, no meaningful resort prior to jihad that Hamas can try.

Hamas's 13th article in their charter can thus be interpreted not necessarily as a rejection of the last-resort principle but as an attempt to apply that principle. Members of Hamas may not have thought that way about last-resort. They may not even have thought about the last-resort principle at all. But, still, it is possible to take Hamas as working within just war theory and then saying that it cannot apply this principle because it is too late. It is too late in the same sense that in 1939 the Poles could not apply the last-resort principle after the Germans began to occupy their land.

It should be obvious that Hamas's stance on last resort is not the only one possible. Because Fatah, at times at least, does not insist on a complete takeover of Israeli territory, it has room to negotiate. Again, it might not avail itself of the last-resort principle and actually engage in negotiations. But for them negotiations as a series of resorts short of jihad is something they can consider. It is not as if because some factions of Hamas also engage in terrorism that they are precluded from appealing to resorts short of jihad.

Pretty much the same thing can be said of the other principles of just war theory that terrorists tend to treat lightly. Just as it is possible for terrorists (viewed as rebels) to satisfy the just cause and last-resort principles, they can, if they put their minds to it, satisfy most of the other principles. They can, if they wish, develop proportionality arguments that show that their goal (establishing, for example, a true and permanent Muslim state or world order) brings about more good than the harm that war does. They can also argue without great difficulty that their intentions are good. As noted already, they may have trouble with the legitimate authority principle. The problem here is that it is difficult for rebel groups to give meaning to legitimacy. Since few if any nations or groups recognize most rebel groups as legitimate, what does it mean for a group to say that it is legitimate? It sounds like a hollow claim.

A different problem faces rebel groups when they stare the likelihood of success principle in the face. Since many of these groups are small and not very well organized, any estimates of their future success border on fantasy. *— Not thought nec. for Self defense*

Even so, it appears that terrorist groups can, in principle, meet or bypass most of the *ad bellum* criteria that just war theory presents. Some groups may not actually meet these criteria; instead, they may flout them. But it is not impossible for them to meet the criteria. Just because they become terrorists, either immediately or later, does not keep them from making claims that they are operating within the moral realm when it comes to starting a war or struggle. That is, logically it is not a self-contradiction to admit that one is a terrorist and yet claim that one is satisfying many of the *jus ad bellum* principles. The realm of terrorism and ethics are not necessarily incompatible with one another, as some people claim. There is no incompatibility at least in so far as the *jus ad bellum* principles are concerned.

In bello arguments

Revenge

Turning now to the *in bello* side of just war theory, terrorists have a slew of arguments to justify their terrorism. One of these is the revenge argument that can be expressed as 'Do unto others *because* they do it unto you and *as* they do unto you.' This argument needs *as motive* to be distinguished from the motive of revenge discussed in Chapter 6. Talk of motives in that context deals with the psychology of terrorism. That is, it deals with how Palestinians, Afghans, Chechens, Tamils, etc. actually react when they experience, view or read vivid accounts of enemy atrocities. In contrast, *as moral right* justifying revenge presents arguments aimed at showing that revenge is a morally acceptable response. The following passage does not actually present such an argument, but it hints at how that argument might go. Its author is Ayman Al-Zawahiri.

> It [the Coalition of Islamic Fundamentalists] ... is ready for revenge against the heads of the world's gathering of infidels, the United States, Russia, and Israel. It is anxious to seek retribution for the blood of the martyrs, the grief of the mothers, the deprivation of the orphans, the suffering of the detainees, and the scores of the tortured people throughout the land of Islam, from eastern Turkestan to Andalusia [the Islamic state in Spain that ended in 1492] ...[7]

Justice, it seems, requires a response equal or perhaps proportional to the crime. Either way, justice will be harsh simply because the crimes being responded to are so atrocious. Thus, terrorists will not be moved when they are accused of committing hideous deeds. They will reply by saying 'You brought these horrors upon yourselves; you are getting back what you deserve.'

Retaliation is closely related to revenge (and retribution). The main difference is that while revenge is backward-looking, retaliation is forward-looking. Its intent is to stop future bad behaviour of the enemy. By retaliating one tells the enemy, 'We will stop doing what we did, if you, who started it, will stop.' The following passage that quotes Fawzi Barhum, a Hamas spokesman, makes this point clearly. It refers to orders issued by the Israeli prime minister, Ehud Olmert, to his forces to target resistance activists who fire at Israeli settlements.

> 'We warn the IOA [the Israeli Occupation Army] of any such foolishness', he said, adding that Palestinian resistance factions are entitled to retaliate to each Israeli violation. 'However, if Olmert carried out his threat then the calm will be over', he cautioned.[8]

This passage refers to a threat of retaliation rather than retaliation itself. Still, Barhum makes it clear that he considers retaliation as an acceptable option when he tells us that Hamas is *entitled* to retaliate. Evidently, for him, even though retaliating causes harm, it counts as a tactic that does more good than harm when all things are considered.

The family of revenge concepts points to one basic kind of justification for terrorism. A second basic kind follows the concept usually referred to as military necessity. Terrorists, it is said, have no choice but to ply their trade of fear and terror. In the Second World War the British found themselves in a similar 'no choice' situation (see Chapter 3). They were keen on harming the Germans at a time when they could do little else but engage in terror bombing. Mainly the problem was that technology was not up to the task. Bombing at night with what we today call 'dumb' bombs, what harm they could do could only centre on the civilian population. Modern terrorists claim that they are similarly technologically deprived. Not possessing the heavy and sophisticated equipment of their enemies, they have no choice but to employ light and less sophisticated equipment, such as rifles, rocket-propelled grenades and portable bombs.

Compounding the disadvantage of technology is the disadvantage in numbers. Almost always terrorists are outnumbered in their struggles with their enemies. A straight fight between terrorists and their enemies is rarely 'one on one'. It is more like ten or 20 to one. Given these odds, the only choice terrorists have is to engage in a style of guerrilla warfare where terrorism is rarely employed, if at all, or to engage in terrorism pure and simple. Actually they have one other choice. They can fight by combining their guerrilla war and terrorism. Many so-called terrorist groups do adopt this combination strategy. Still, the overall claim is that terrorists have very few options, and thus they are forced into engaging in terrorism.

Like revenge that has retaliation closely attached to it, necessity has a close tie to success. The success argument goes something like this. As noted, terrorist options are limited. In one sense, that is unfortunate. 'We terrorists', they might say, 'would have preferred to be able to attack the enemy in other ways and, as a result, not do so much harm to innocents. But in another sense, we are fortunate. The only main tactic available to us turns out to be surprisingly powerful.' In a piece of writing entitled 'Why Attack America?' Al-Zawahiri discusses the methods of fighting that he thinks the '*muhahid* Islamic movement' should adopt in its jihad against the West. These include methods that those that will inflict maximum casualties on the enemy over the long haul, those that employ martyr tactics (since they are so effective), and those that permit the *mujahidin* to use any and all weapons to get the job done.[9]

What he says is interesting for several reasons. First, it praises the success-rate of 'martyr operations'. Presumably non-martyr operations are also successful but martyr operations are, one might say, the best of the best. Second, in speaking of martyr operations, Al-Zawahiri avoids admitting that he is sponsoring, encouraging or even participating in terrorist operations. Instead he talks of jihad, fighting the 'Crusader–Jewish alliance', and thus liberating Islamic countries and peoples. Third, success is measured incrementally. Good as terrorist tactics are, Al-Zawahiri recognizes that they work best only if the Islamic fundamentalists are patient. They must not expect sudden miracles. Fourth, success is also measured in terms of deterring immoral influences. Fifth, Islamists see themselves as the victims in the struggle. If they are successful in their operations their success will take place within the realm of ethics. This last point is certainly not new. In fact, it is implicit or explicit in just about all the writings of the radical Islamists.

The third basic argument used by terrorists in defence of what they do is quite different from the other two. Both the revenge and the necessity arguments have a place for regret. Those using these arguments can say that they regret having to harm large groups of innocent people. Nonetheless they can also say that they have good reasons for causing this harm. In effect, what they are doing is making exceptions to the principle of discrimination. But, they say, their exceptions are morally justified. Overall what they do is right even if part of what they do is, regretfully, wrong.

In contrast, the third argument has little room for regret. That argument goes something like this:

The leaders of the 'evil' nations as well as their military establishment are responsible for the horrible things they do. If they occupy another nation, kill many people, create economic chaos they are subject to retribution. They should pay for their crimes with their lives. But especially in democratic countries, the people are not innocent. These not-so-innocent people vote for their 'evil' leaders, support these leaders by paying taxes, support them by defending their actions, and cheer for them. In doing all these things, these people, usually the majority, become responsible for the actions of their nation. They can be blamed; and beyond that, they can be attacked. It is not a violation of the principle of discrimination to use terrorist tactics against them. So when terrorists attack a shopping centre or a bus they are not doing something morally awful the way it is sometimes portrayed in the mass media of the 'evil' nations. If regret has a place in these attacks it has to do with the harm done to children. They are innocent as are perhaps prisoners in the 'evil' nation. But the harm done to children is unavoidable. It counts as collateral damage: a concept all too familiar to the military establishment of the evil nations. Still, given the cause that the terrorists are fighting for, the regret that goes with killing a few, or even not so few, children is overridden by the steps the terrorists take to further their glorious moral cause. And concerning these steps, there is no room for regret.

Conclusions concerning non-state terrorism

Terrorists tell us that critics of terrorism make a pervasive logical error in assessing what terrorists do. The critics focus narrowly on the actions of the terrorists. Thus what they see are horrible events. They see death, suffering and physical destruction. What they do not see is any logic or order to what is happening. So to them, terrorism seems irrational, senseless, crazy and beyond comprehension.

What the critics need to do, the terrorists say, is broaden their view of events. Once the critics look at the whole picture, they cannot help but see that some terrorist acts are a response (by way of revenge, retribution, retaliation) to past events instigated by 'evil' governments, their military establishments and the paramilitary groups that they sponsor. Others are a response to the present environment in which terrorists are forced to operate. Given that they are technologically disadvantaged, the ways they can fight are extremely limited (military necessity). Still other acts are a response to the realization that the government and military elite of 'evil' nations are not the only ones responsible for the evil they do (collective responsibility).

Once the full picture is viewed, terrorism can no longer be seen as a senseless and totally immoral activity. Those who engage in it are now seen as rational people desperately fighting for a moral cause. They fight within the framework of the *jus ad bellum* principles *and* the *in bello* principles.

Arguing for state terrorism

Justifying state terrorism is not an easy task. In large part this is because states, more than non-state groups, have the power to do more harm. Non-state terrorist groups recognize this fact. They regularly complain that they get bad publicity for their 'unspeakable crimes' even though their 'crimes' are much smaller in scale than those that states perpetrate.

Still, a plausible case for state terrorism can be made in certain situations. We have already reviewed one such situation. The British bombing of German cities *early in the war* seems justified given the desperate straits both Britain and the USSR found themselves in at that time (see Chapter 3). Later, as the Allies became more powerful, the justification for this bombing was somewhat less. But for a while, the case for terror bombing seemed to be there.

A plausible case for state terrorism can be made for a quite different Second World War scenario. Late in that war, in Asia, the Americans were faced with the prospect of carrying out a very costly invasion of Japan. Unlike the British, who worried that they might very well lose the war unless they resorted to terror bombing, the Americans knew by 1945 that they would win. For them, the only questions were when and how they would win, and at what cost. Mainly they were thinking of cost to themselves, but the costs in Japanese lives (and property) were also in the minds of some. When the atomic bombs became available, the option of using these weapons became real. If they were used, the Americans conjectured that the Japanese would quickly capitulate. If then one or two such bombs were dropped, Japanese casualties could run between 100,000 and 300,000, while American casualties would be zero. If, instead, the invasion took place, Japanese casualties could run into a million or more, and American casualties into hundreds of thousands.[10] Given their way of fighting, the Japanese death-rate among those who would be counted as casualties would be much higher than for the Americans. Even so, an estimate of 30,000–50,000 or more American deaths was realistic.

Faced with causing a grossly disproportionately larger number of casualties by not dropping the bombs on Japanese cities, dropping the bombs seemed to be a plausible (moral) option. Complicating the issue of what should and should not have been done in 1945 is the claim that the Americans had other options available besides dropping the bomb on Japanese cities and invading Japan. Two such options were that they could have dropped a demonstration bomb, *options* or they could have blockaded Japan until it capitulated (perhaps in 1946). For the sake of showing that there are conceivable situations where state terrorism can be defended, we are assuming that these additional options were not present or, in the end, could not have been defended (e.g. because if the Japanese were not impressed enough with a demonstration bombing in Tokyo harbour to end the war, the US would have had only one operational bomb left to make an impression). The argument then comes down as follows. If state terrorism, costly as it is, is less costly than a policy of non-terrorism, then state terrorism is justified.

An interesting feature of these arguments concerned with British and American bombings is how rare are the situations where they can be applied. They are so rare that one is hard pressed to imagine additional plausible cases. On the state level, exceptions to the principle of discrimination are just hard to come by. It follows that most cases of state terrorism, for example, as practised by the Turks (against the Armenians in 1916), Hitler, Stalin and the Sudanese government (against the people in Darfur), are unjustified.

9   Arguments against Terrorism

The previous chapter could have been called 'Arguments from the Terrorist Point of View'. Although many arguments in that chapter reflect the terrorist point of view, the real source of these arguments is not someone's viewpoint, but just war theory. That chapter looked at the arguments that terrorists (or anybody else) might present to justify terrorist activity. Similarly, this chapter could have been called 'Arguments from the Point of View of the Victims of Terrorism'. Were that the case, the arguments would be highly emotional and difficult to understand. Rather, the arguments in this chapter are again derived from just war theory, even though many of them do, in fact, reflect the point of view of the victims of terrorism.

But if just war theory is to generate a series of arguments against terrorism, a review of the theory will serve to remind us what its principles are. The review is especially useful since many of the points made in this study suggest that the theory needs to be modified in certain respects. (This became evident in the previous chapter where much was said about the differences between wars fought between states and those fought between states and non-state groups.)

As described in Chapter 1, the original version of the just war theory divides into two parts with the first part dealing with how wars are supposed to start (*jus ad bellum* – justice of the war). That part has six principles which are primarily addressed to states (nations). Briefly, here again are the six principles:

1. *Just cause* States (nations) are supposed to go to war only if they have at least one good reason for doing so. Roughly speaking, that good reason has to do with aggression. States are permitted to respond to some form of aggression (or to a humanitarian disaster), but not to initiate war for gain, plunder, etc.

2. *Good intentions* The intentions of states are supposed to be in accordance with the just cause principle. Thus a state's intentions in going to war should be aimed at countering aggression, not, for example, at expanding its empire.

3. *Likelihood of success* States should enter a war only if they have a real prospect of some sort of success. States should not enter a war if it is a hopeless venture.

4. *Proportionality* Although the costs of war are high, the benefits (freedom, etc.) should be higher. These measurements are estimates made *before* the war starts. 'Second-guess' measurements taking account of what is learned after the war starts or after it is over are irrelevant to the application of this (and the previous) principle.

5. *Last resort* Wars should not be entered into precipitously. A series of steps should be tried before states enter into violent conflict.

6. *Legitimate authority* Certain individuals or groups have a monopoly on war. Only they (e.g. national legislatures, supreme councils, dictators) can properly start a war. If others (e.g. regional chiefs) start a war, that war is said not to be legitimate. The UN is seen by many as a legitimate authority, especially with regard to wars fought for humanitarian reasons. However, the United States does not accept the jurisdiction of the UN and with override its decisions.

The second part of the theory deals with the prosecution of the war (*jus in bello* – justice in the war). There are two principles here.

1. *Proportionality* In the war, proportionality refers to the expected benefits and costs of *battles* and *campaigns*: not the *war* itself.

2. *Discrimination* Non-combatants ('innocents') in the war should not be targeted. Participants can be targeted.

As we have seen in the previous chapter (and some earlier ones) the classic just war theory does not really apply when the war or struggle is not between nations (states). When that war is between a nation and a non-nation (non-state) group, some of the principles do not fit well. This being so, we are proposing that just war theory be modified so that it becomes two separate theories. One theory leaves things as they are, and this works well enough when the struggle is between two or more states. We will call this theory, Theory C. The second theory concerns conflicts between state and non-state entities. We will call this new theory, Theory N. Theory N resembles Theory C, but differs in certain important respects.

Theory N

preliminary duty

Just cause This is the same as in Theory C, but with one exception. In certain circumstances, states can *prevent* non-state attacks in a way that is not allowed when they deal with potential attacks from other states. Prevention is allowed for at least three reasons. First, non-state groups have probably already attacked the state in the past. So to attack them prevents not a first, but a second or third attack. Second, non-state groups gather weapons non-contingently. That is, they do so as the first step of an attack that is actually forthcoming. Normally they do not gather weapons in the way that nations do. Nations *do not* gather weapons in order to start a war, but they do so on the possibility that a war might start. Third, non-state groups are dangerous and difficult to locate. Nations may be dangerous, but they are not difficult to locate. If by some lucky chance non-state terrorist groups are found, it seems foolish to miss out on the opportunity to harm them.

Right intentions Theory N's version of this principle is the same as Theory C's.

Likelihood of success Generally speaking, non-state groups are exempt from meeting the requirements of this principle. Since it is almost impossible for them to make rational calculations of success in the distant future, they are not expected to make such calculations. At the same time, states involved in the struggle have to satisfy this principle just as they do when they are contemplating going to war with other states. Being well-formed structures, states can always assess their resources and make at least crude calculations about their likelihood of success.

Proportionality Both sides have to satisfy this principle. Even a non-state group should be able to articulate what is the greater good of its revolutions (should it succeed) and then measure that good against the costs of a protracted war.

Last resort This principle changes under Theory N for the states involved in a war with non-state groups. In certain circumstances, states (e.g. when non-state groups have attacked months earlier and may attack in the future) may attack their non-state group opponents. Both sides might try some other options, but if states happen to find their stealthy opponents in the middle of preparations to resume the war, they are justified in making a preventive strike.

Legitimate authority Non-state groups need not satisfy this principle for the simple reason that it is impossible for them to do so. These groups may have powerful leaders, but their leaders usually lack *legitimacy*. Self-proclamations of legitimacy are not enough. Legitimacy comes when other nations and/or large non-state groups officially recognize non-state groups. Any one non-nation group may become legitimate over a period of time but, in the meantime, much of its struggle with a state will have taken place before legitimacy has been established.

Justice in the war (jus in bello)

Both the proportionality and the discrimination principle apply in Theory N as they did in Theory C.

Jus ad bellum criticism

The terrorist case for satisfying the just cause principle is stronger than it first seems. That is one of the conclusions of the previous chapter. Rebel (non-state) groups that practise terrorism, either full- or part-time, often have much to complain about. They, along with the larger ethnic, religious or social group that they represent, are often severely abused and exploited. At best, then, arguments against terrorists with respect to just cause can only aim at identifying the exaggeration, distortion and other forms of deception found in terrorist rhetoric. But, after these forms of deception have been discounted, many complaints still remain. There are too many injustices in the world for this not to be so. It appears, then, that (most) terrorists find themselves on the right side of the just cause principle. They can, and often do, satisfy this just war theory principle.

At first glance, the last-resort principle also does not appear to be on the terrorist side. Terrorists, it can be argued, are too quick to start doing their dirty work. Being moved by their cause, they lack the patience required to take the many steps (e.g. negotiations) required before reaching last resort.

There is another reason for supposing that terrorists normally do not meet the standards of this principle. When we speak of terrorists we tend to use expressions such as 'the terrorists' or 'the insurgents'. This tempts us to think of the insurgents and/or the terrorists as if they were a single entity. It is as if we were talking of 'the British', 'The Germans', 'the marines', or 'the army'. But terrorist and/or insurgent groups fighting in any one area of the world are often not a single entity. Rather, they are made up of several groups, with each group having its own leader and agenda. So to speak of 'an insurgency' or 'the insurgency' is convenient but may be misleading. It would be better to speak of insurgencies or various groups of insurgents or terrorists.

If that is right, it becomes obvious why the last-resort principle will be difficult to apply. How does anyone determine when (speaking misleadingly) the insurgency has failed to meet the last-resort principle? Has it failed when one group of insurgents starts terrorizing people? What if a second group starts fighting a guerrilla-style war but does not employ the tactic of terrorism? In contrast to making a judgement that a single entity such as a nation has met or failed to meet the last-resort principle, it seems difficult at best to make a judgement about a group of insurgencies succeeding or failing to meet that principle.

Of these two objections to terrorists meeting the last resort principle, the first, having to do with impatience, can be dealt with quickly. It is true that members of an insurgency and/or terrorist group are an impatient lot. Many are young, convinced completely of the rightness of their cause and anxious to prove to themselves and to others how brave they are. But it is also true that others in the history of the conflict that the impatient ones find themselves in have taken steps toward satisfying the last-resort principle. Over time, less radical groups have tried negotiations, boycotts, demonstrations, etc. And, as is often the case, these steps have failed. So although the insurgents and/or terrorists themselves have not taken a series of steps to satisfy the last-resort principle, others may well have done so on their behalf. This being so, we can say that a particular insurgent and/or terrorist group has satisfied the standards of that principle because it stands in an historical line that has met these standards.

The second objection concerns diversity. How can anyone determine when the last-resort principle has or has not been satisfied when we are dealing with several groups? Making a determination in this circumstance seems impossible, but in fact it is not. It is done by dealing with each group individually. Once Group A is identified (often no easy task), judgements are made. Did it (e.g. Hamas in Palestine, al Sadr's Mahdi army in Iraq) start the fighting and/or the terrorism? Did it break the truce? Did it call for a ceasefire and then cease hostilities? There are, of course, complications.

Fighting starts and it is not clear whether Group A, B or C is responsible since, in part, no group may want to admit publicly that it is responsible. Still, in many cases, responsibility can be assigned. When it is, we see the last-resort principle at work, piecemeal, as it were.

So there is no insurmountable obstacle to having insurgency groups and terrorist groups meet the last-resort principle. And, as we have seen, many of them meet the last-resort principle's standards thanks to the patience of their predecessors. But now what of the other *jus ad bellum* principles? Can terrorists, insurgent groups, revolutionaries, etc. meet, for example, the good intentions principle? Briefly, no objections can be raised to keep them from doing so. Again, many terrorists may not in fact meet the standards of this principle. But many will, if for no other reason than that these groups are filled with young idealists who are all too happy to fight and die for their cause.

What of the proportionality principle? It has already been admitted that this principle is difficult to apply – in any war setting. Predicting the benefits and costs of war is filled with uncertainty. One would suppose that predicting the outcome of an insurgency war or struggle would involve even greater uncertainty.

However, if the difficulty were such that no assessment could be made, that would not show that the terrorists had failed to satisfy this principle. It could not be argued that terrorists had started a struggle in order to generate costs that were greater than the benefits. Instead, they would have started a war or struggle in which no one could calculate the benefits and costs. This amounts to saying that the principle has no application for insurgents and terrorists. They simply would not have to meet its standards. In effect, under Theory N, proportionality has the same status as does likelihood of success.

The other possibility is that, in spite of all the difficulties, some assessments can be made. If that possibility were real, many insurgents could argue (as in the previous chapter) that their war effort might in principle do more good than harm. So either the proportionality principle is one that insurgents and terrorists can ignore or, in principle, satisfy. There is, then, no reason to suppose that they must violate this principle.

It appears, then, that in their application of *jus ad bellum* principles of just war theory terrorists can, but do not necessarily, act justly. We have already argued that the principles of legitimate authority and likelihood of success do not apply to them (Theory N). Likewise, it may be that the proportionality principle does not apply to them. But *if* it does, they can meet that principle's standards. Similarly, they can meet the standards of last resort, good intentions and just cause.

If one is to show that terrorists and insurgents act immorally, it appears, then, that that showing cannot be on the level of *jus ad bellum*. To repeat, they can choose to violate one or more of the *jus ad bellum* principles, but they are not doomed to violating them because of the nature of their enterprise. Rather, just as they can choose to violate these principles, they can choose not to.

Jus in bello criticism

If there is nothing morally wrong, at least in principle, with terrorist (and insurgent) behaviour on the *jus ad bellum* side of just war theory, the wrongness (if it is present) must be on the *in bello* side. That should surprise no one since most of the complaints we hear about terrorism concerns its treatment of 'innocents'. It is the principle of discrimination that terrorists allegedly violate.

However, as we discovered in the previous chapter, terrorists deny they are in violation. They do not deny that they attack, kill and maim so-called innocents. But they deny that their attacks are unjust. Terrorists have (as we have noted) three basic arguments to explain why they are still on the side of the angels even though they are shedding much blood. To recap: (1) they take revenge on the immoral behaviour of their enemies; (2) they attack 'innocents' in self-defence in situations where they cannot act otherwise (the necessity argument); and (3) they insist that so-called innocents are not really innocent (argument from collective responsibility).

We shall deal with these arguments in reverse order because the collective responsibility argument holds one of the important keys to understanding the other two.

Notice that most terrorists do not directly deny the validity of the discrimination principle. We can see this in their vehement complaints about how *their* children, *their* mothers, *their* grandparents, that is, *their* 'innocents' are killed, maimed and abused. Acts against their 'innocents' are said to be not just wrong, but outrageously wrong. Sheikh Muhammad Sayyed Tantawi argues that while divine laws do not approve the killing of children, old people, and peaceful citizens, but that those doing suicide operations are 'in a state of legitimate self-defense against those who attack them and do not show mercy to old people, children, or women'.[1] A group calling itself the World Islamic Front tells us that 'despite the great devastation inflicted upon the Iraqi people by the crusader–Zionist alliance, and despite the huge number of those killed, which has exceeded one million … despite all this, the Americans are once again trying to repeat the horrific massacres'.[2] Having listed its complaints, the Front goes on to issue a *fatwa*. Muslims are commanded to attack the Americans and their allies, no matter whether they have military or civilian status.

These and similar terrorist claims that place their own people under the protection of the principle of discrimination but do not extend this protection to their enemies are logically flawed. The flaw lies in the so-called universalizability principle.[3] That principle tells us that we should act consistently in making moral (ethical) judgements. It tells us to treat people who are alike, alike. If our children are immune from attack, then your children (since they are like ours) should also be immune. If the children of the people the terrorists belong to are immune from attack, their enemy's children should also be immune. The same point applies to mothers, grandparents, doctors, religious leaders, tailors, book salesmen, etc. If one side's grandparents are immune, so are the other side's grandparents.

It is at this point that terrorists insert their collective responsibility argument into their case for practising terrorism. They say that their grandparents are not really like their enemy's grandparents. Their own are truly innocent and so retain their immunity from attack, while their enemies' are not truly innocent and so do not retain immunity. Their argument, then, is that although they respect the principle of discrimination, they are justified in making their enemies' grandparents. exceptions to that principle.

In order to reply to this argument in its effort to deflect the application of the universalizability principle, it is necessary to look at terrorist rhetoric once again. In the previous chapter that rhetoric was discounted for the sake of uncovering the kernel of truth of the claims made by terrorists that their people are being killed and exploited. But now the discounted rhetoric assumes a new importance since it is used by the terrorists to protect their own innocents while attacking the alleged innocents of their enemies. If that rhetoric misrepresents the facts, that misrepresentation needs to be exposed.

Speaking in terms that apply to a wide variety of wars, struggles, etc., a proper representation looks something like this:

Many enemies of the terrorists can also make a plausible case for having just cause on their side. They too can claim that they have entered the war with justice on their side. They too can mount complaints about how their people have been mistreated. (Think here how Jews living outside Israel have often been mistreated. Or how Russians living in Chechnya, Buddhists in Sri Lanka and Shiites in the Sunni part of Iraq have been mistreated.)

It may seem paradoxical that both sides can be on the right side of justice. This seems so especially if one thinks of certain clearcut cases of right and wrong such as Germany's invasion of Poland in 1939 and its invasion of the USSR in 1941. But the issues dividing nations, on one side, and groups, on the other, are often not clearcut. In such settings, convincing arguments showing that both sides are 'in the right' can be presented. No doubt, the participants in the struggle won't see the justice of the other side. That is where the rhetoric on both sides does its damage. It blinds. But if one steps back away from the struggle, one sees that the issues dividing people are more complicated than the rhetoric on each side allows.

Better vision thus forces a change in the terrorists' argument. They can no longer easily discount the lives of the 'innocents' on the other side. If there is a level of justice on both sides, then killing the enemy's innocents is comparable to the enemy killing the innocents on the terrorist side. If it is wrong to kill terrorist innocents, it must be wrong to kill the innocents of their enemies. Or, putting it in positive terms, if it is right to maintain the immunity from attack of the terrorists' people, it is right to maintain the immunity of their enemies' people.

A completely different argument leads to the same conclusion: namely, that terrorists cannot, as easily as they suppose, justify their attacks on enemy 'innocents'. This argument focuses on the meaning of terms like 'innocent' and 'participants in war', and on 'the principle of discrimination' itself. It has the advantage over the previous argument of applying to all, not just many, situations where terrorism is practised.

The historical intent of the discrimination principle was to constrain the slaughter of war. Once a war started, the most obvious way to do that was (and is) to restrict those with arms from attacking those without arms. Yet, as the principle came to be applied, it was clear to all that many of those without arms were sympathetic to and even supportive of those with arms. The British people support, and are expected to support, their armed forces. It is the same with the Germans, the Russians and the Chinese. Some of these supporters might even have a close relationship with their military, so their immunity to attack would come into question. Munitions workers are an example here. But being married to a soldier, or engaged to be married to a sailor, or the daughter of an airman is not sufficient grounds, to invalidate one's immunity.

But when terrorists present their collective responsibility argument they, in effect, change the meaning of 'innocent' within the context of the discrimination principle. The circle of those who count as innocent is made so small that it becomes almost impossible for any adult member of the enemy population to claim immunity. The slightest contact with the war effort (e.g. as with citizens who voted to support a leader who later decided to go to war against the terrorists) is enough to throw them out of the safe circle of the innocent. Even those in the enemy camp who do not support the war on terrorism are not immune from attack. After all, they could have done more to prevent that war from starting. To be innocent now means that one must be completely uncontaminated.

The change in meaning of 'innocent' that terrorists present has important consequences. Arguments can be won and lost by the manipulation of meaning. By narrowing the meaning of 'innocent', terrorists can 'prove' that only children and a few others are immune from attack. They can 'prove', in addition, that they are acting in accordance with the principle of discrimination even though they are killing secretaries, shop-assistants, housewives, boot-blacks and so on.

Because meaning-manipulation can have these effects, we expect those who change the meaning of terms to explain themselves. The explanations of terrorists are inadequate. It is not enough for them to say, 'The majority of the enemy voted to support the war' because that reason was already discounted by the discrimination principle as traditionally understood. (One's involvement in war had to be greater than giving support to one's country's political institutions.) Nor is it enough to claim that people lose immunity because they encourage soldiers (of their own nation) in their fighting. That kind of behaviour is to be expected. As a result, those who formulated the discrimination principle, and those who used it in the past, have argued that cheering one's own husband on as he goes to battle does not force a woman to forfeit her immunity to attack.

In other words, there is no rationale for narrowing the meaning of 'innocent' and thus radically changing the discrimination principle. The reasons many terrorists give for the change are not reasons at all. Instead, they represent a direct and unexplained denial of the principle as it has been understood over the years and in many cultures. Thus, as we have so far examined it, the collective responsibility argument offers the terrorists little help in justifying their attacks on 'soft' targets. So terrorists' behaviour with respect to 'soft' targets remains a major flaw in their claim that their wars or struggles are fought within the bounds of ethics. The way in which they deal with the discrimination principle throws them out-of-bounds.

But there is still another argument that shows that the meaning argument is flawed. It makes use of the universalizability argument once again. Grant for the moment that 'innocent' has the narrow meaning that some terrorists claim it has. By this narrow meaning, terrorists can justify an attack against almost anyone they please among the enemy civilian population and have no guilt in doing so. But if they can attack the enemy population because it supports its own troops, the enemy can turn the argument round and say that the terrorists' population can be attacked because, in one way or another, it supports the terrorists. The two populations are too much alike for the terrorist argument to take hold. So if the terrorists continue to insist that they are justified in attacking their enemies' populations, they can no longer blame their enemies for attacking their 'innocent' populations. Either that, or they must give up attacking their enemies' civilian population if they want to stay (as they claim they do) within the moral realm.

However, terrorists need not abandon all of the meaning version of the collective responsibility argument quite yet. There are special situations, they argue, where collective responsibility still holds even if they (reluctantly) concede that in most situations (like those discussed above) their argument fails to support their position. The situations they have in mind are of two kinds. The first has to do with Israel. That country has a reserve, rather than a standing, military establishment. Israel literally can't afford to keep a large military in the field on an everyday basis. So it trains its military personnel, and then sends them home to be bakers, carpenters, teachers, shop-owners and nurses. Periodically, all these young people come back to camp for refresher courses and training in the field. But, again, they go home when they finish their new training sessions and take on the status of being in the ready reserve.

all are reserve soldiers

This sort of Israeli military establishment encourages terrorists to argue that when one of their martyr terrorists attacks a coffee shop in Jerusalem, she is not attacking innocents. These young people, or at least a good number of them, are in the military, albeit out of uniform. Since these young people are not innocents, attacking them does not violate even the traditional version of the principle of discrimination.

Answ.

How is one to reply to such an argument? Well, the bombed coffee shop is not a military target even if reservists are enjoying themselves there. Further, the terrorists cannot claim that they know that most of those in the shop are reservists: probably most are not. So the terrorists' argument is factually as well as logically flawed. But even if most of those at the shop are reservists, they are civilians first and reservists second. Their lives are dominated, day-in, day-out, by their civilian work and their family responsibilities. To be sure, they can don their military uniforms and show up at the front. But civilian supporters of terrorists can do the same thing. It is true that most of these supporters are not actually members of any terrorist group. But they can join quickly and easily, and then they can get themselves fitted with a bomb-belt almost as quickly as the Israeli reservists can climb into their tanks. The terrorists thus cannot use the reservist version of the collective responsibility argument without making it possible for the Israelis to apply a similar argument against them. Or, what amounts to the same thing: if it is wrong to kill innocents on the terrorist side, it is wrong to kill innocents on the Israeli side.

The second kind of situation that might tempt terrorists not to give up on the collective responsibility argument ran its course in

Algeria during the 1950s revolution. At that time, the insurgents treated those French citizens who had settled in Algeria as 'occupiers'. They were thought of as occupiers in much the same sense that the French troops serving in Algeria were occupiers. The logic of using the term 'occupier' is obvious. If the occupier soldiers can be justly attacked, so can the occupier settlers.

This insurgency/terrorist argument is weaker than the one used against the Israelis. It could be argued that the Israeli reservists pose a long-term threat to the terrorists even if (because they are at home) they pose no short-term threat. But the settlers pose neither a long- nor a short-term (military) threat to the insurgents. They are civilians pure and simple and so should be protected by the principle of discrimination.

The terrorist version of their second major argument, the revenge argument, says that revenge is a just move against an enemy that has perpetrated gross wrongs against a totally innocent people. The argument has a ring of plausibility to it. But like the collective responsibility argument, revenge falls foul of the universalizability principle. It is a tactic that notoriously taints both sides. It is often impossible to determine which side started the violence that is to be avenged. After a while, it becomes tit-for-tat. Nonetheless, one side, and then the other, often fails to see the mutual tainting because it focuses on the enemy's last awful act and the one before that. Aided by rhetoric, each side thinks that it, and it alone, is right in seeking revenge. But any reasonable application of the universalizability principle shows that revenge is an immoral practice. Neither side would accept it as a way of fighting if each side realized that the revenge command is 'Let us harm them the way they harmed us, and let others harm us the way we have harmed them.'

The terrorist version of the retribution argument cannot be used to justify terrorism for a different reason. To act retributively is to punish someone who has committed some sort of crime. But typically, terrorists do not punish just the perpetrators of the crime. Their attacks are often not especially aimed at the perpetrators at all.

Instead, they are aimed at the general population. That sort of retribution would make sense only if it were granted that the meaning of 'innocent' were narrowed in a way that we have just argued is not legitimate. Once the terrorists' meaning-manipulation is exposed, it is clear that what they call retribution is not really retribution at all. Most of the victims of their attacks still belong to the class of those who are innocent.

The last argument terrorists use to justify their terrorist practices is necessity. We cannot help acting as we do, they say, because we are at a military (technological) disadvantage. What works best for us in overcoming our disadvantage is terrorism. It alone is the tactic that significantly gives support to our cause.

A critical look at this argument has to concede the following. Terrorism, especially when it aims at so-called 'soft' targets, is a very effective tactic for non-state groups. There is no question but that by following this tactic these groups have caused much more disorder throughout the world than anyone would have supposed a generation ago. Given the great short-term effect of terrorism, it is no wonder that terrorists have come to believe in the necessity argument. They suppose that if they are to further their cause, and further it in the quickest possible time, it is necessary that they do what they do.

However, conceding the point about terrorism's success is not the same as conceding the validity of the necessity argument. That argument does not merely say that if terrorists are supposed to win quickly, it is necessary to use terrorism over against other tactics. Rather, it says that there are no other tactics available for engaging in their struggle. In effect, according to the argument, the only choice that rebels have is to employ terrorism or abandon their cause.

If that is what the necessity argument tells us, then it is a bad argument. It is not the case that in many insurgency wars there are no other options but terrorism. We can appreciate this point by imagining what might have happened in the Iraq war of 2003 if the insurgents had gone out of their way to avoid killing innocent civilians. Instead of detonating their bombs in shopping centres, mosques and crowded streets, let us suppose they had aimed at the invading military forces, or the Iraqi police and military personnel, or government officials working cooperatively with the invasion forces. In aiming at these targets, they would have been engaging in a kind of guerrilla war and would have needed to employ only limited terrorist tactics.

Had they fought in this way, it is not clear that they would have been less successful than they have been so far. They might even have been more successful. Their specific targeting might have offended fewer Iraqis and so increased their chances of winning the hearts and minds of the population as a whole.

The same point can be made with regard to the Provisional IRA. They found that when they pursued more radical terrorist tactics, such as bombing civilians, they lost the support of their own people. Other options were open to the Provisionals, and eventually they chose them.

The Greek rebels (terrorists) of the 1970s and 1980s made the same choice (see Chapter 3). Although they were not successful in their long-term goal of reforming the government, they did show that when terrorism avoids attacks on 'innocents' they can survive and also they can experience a great deal of tactical success.

Matters are not so different in Israel/Palestine/Lebanon. Hamas, Hezbollah and other groups opposed to Israel have other choices than to fire rockets into Israel in an indiscriminate fashion, and to send suicide bombers into coffee houses and buses so as to kill anyone and everyone. They could aim their rockets at military and police facilities, and use bombs to attack Israeli infrastructure (e.g. bridges, railways, and government buildings). More care and planning would be required in making such attacks, but it is not obvious that such attacks would be ineffective. It is also not obvious that employing such tactics is impossible in many other insurgency wars. Thus it doesn't appear to be true that insurgents are forced to use terror tactics. Because of the asymmetry in weaponry, their choices are somewhat limited. But they are rarely limited to the point that they have no choice but to resort to terrorism against soft targets.

The mistake that terrorists make in claiming that they have no choice but to fight as they do is more serious than the criticisms of their claims presented so far suggests. This is because the exception to the discrimination principle that they allow themselves to enjoy covers their whole struggle. Recall that when writers such as Michael Walzer said that the British had no choice but to bomb German cities (and so to attack German civilians) the bombing was limited to a time that he called a supreme emergency.[4] Once the British gained more power (and allies in the Soviets and the Americans), and thus were no longer facing such an emergency, the British, he said, could no longer rightly continue their saturation bombing of Hamburg, Cologne, Berlin and other German cities. In contrast, what terrorists claim for themselves is that they should be permitted to attack 'innocents' during the whole war. They are not, they think, to be blamed for attacking 'innocents' from the beginning to the end of their struggle. Thus, if it is a mistake for terrorists to argue that they are morally permitted to attack 'innocents' out of necessity, it is an even greater mistake to argue that they can initiate these attacks in perpetuity. *– but still as long as no other alternative.*

Some brief comments about the principle of proportionality (*in bello*) are appropriate. Because of the cruelty of most terrorist attacks it is tempting to argue that these attacks violate this principle. The harm done seems to outweigh whatever benefits the terrorists claim result from their actions. But this way of thinking flies in the face of the great political and economic effects of terrorism. Terrorism, as Pape reminds us, is not always successful.[5] But it is successful often enough for terrorists to claim that when they make cost/benefits analyses of their future attacks, these analyses will show that their future attacks are in accord with the proportionality principle. In effect, then, terrorists cannot be condemned *en masse* for violating the proportionality principle.

Summary

The reputation that terrorists have makes it seem as if they must be in violation of the whole of just war theory, that they systematically violate each and every principle of that theory. But that is not correct. Terrorists can satisfy all the *jus ad bellum* principles that apply to their way of fighting. Any one terrorist group can fail to meet one or more of these standards of just behaviour. If a group, for example, begins a struggle in a remote region of a nation in order to loot and rape, it would fail to satisfy the just cause and perhaps other principles of just war theory. But other groups are capable of satisfying these *jus ad bellum* principles. These groups can, therefore, quite properly claim that they are fighting from within the moral realm.

Where they depart that realm is in the *in bello* portion of just war theory. They do not depart by violating the principle of proportionality, but rather the principle of discrimination.

At this point terrorists go into denial. They present several reasons for denying their departure. They say that they can rightly seek vengeance, they can rightly apply the notion of collective responsibility to blame almost everyone on their opponents' side, and rightly fight as they do out of necessity. But all of their arguments fail. Most importantly they fail because of the ease with which they discount the status of their enemies. By their rhetoric, their enemies are guilty of crimes so gross that they cannot be excused. Further, they claim that their own people are totally good and their enemies' totally bad. But once their rhetoric is challenged, it becomes clear that the people on both sides of many conflicts are not that different from one another. Roughly speaking, both sides are equally good and equally bad, and so it becomes morally impossible for terrorists to defend their own people while butchering those of their enemies. In effect, terrorists who target 'innocents', deserve all the criticism that they have been receiving, for, in spite of their efforts, they have not uncovered legitimate exceptions to the discrimination principle. Rather, they have violated that principle, and violated it in a most gross fashion.

10 Dealing with Terrorism

It should be clear by now to all except those with their hands over their eyes that there is no quick fix for the problems posed by terrorism. Given that terrorism has been around for a long time, that it has few problems motivating its members and recruiting new ones and that its targets are everywhere, the future points to a difficult and extended bout with the monster.

Although difficult, the task of dealing with terrorism is not impossible. It can be divided into three overlapping sub-tasks. The first has to do with military measures that show some promise for controlling many forms of terrorism. The second concerns non-military steps to be taken outside a nation's borders, while the third has to do with internal measures. Many of these recommendations have already been made. However, there is some merit in putting together under one roof what is found here and there and, as a bonus, adding a few new recommendations. It should be emphasized that some of these recommendations, whether military or not, do not necessarily apply to each and every terrorist campaign. Most, however, can be generally applied, and indeed are general in nature. Their purpose is to focus our attention in a certain direction rather than to make specific recommendations as to how to defeat terrorism. We begin with military recommendations.

Military recommendations

Identifying the enemy and setting goals

Terrorism is not the enemy; terrorists are. All terrorists are not the enemy; only some are. Doing anything and everything to one's enemy should not be one's goal; doing something more specific is. What all this means is that it makes no sense to conduct a worldwide war on terrorism, and then suppose that the phenomenon as a whole can be obliterated on an unconditional-surrender basis. As we have seen, terrorism changes by growing and shrinking, and then popping up in new places. If a nation's goal is to eliminate terrorism everywhere and completely, it is doomed to failure.

However, some success can be achieved by identifying one terrorist group (presumably the most dangerous one around), setting achievable goals such as inflicting serious harm upon it, and then inflicting harm. Having achieved some success in dealing with one group, attention can then be turned to another group. The idea is to deal with one terrorist group at a time. Once one and then a second terrorist group have been harmed, victory should not be declared. Harming terrorism is like harming a generation of weeds. The next generation is likely show up after a while. Instead of making victory claims, preventive steps should be taken to deal with that next generation of weeds.

Good intelligence

Sun Tzu said: 'to remain in ignorance of the enemy's condition, simply because one grudges the outlay of a hundred ounces of silver in honors and emoluments, is the height of inhumanity'.[1] Perhaps the translation should say 'the height of stupidity'. If intelligence is important to the success of campaigns in regular war where the enemy is, relatively speaking, out in the open, it is even more important when one's enemy keeps a stealthy profile.

Although the use of electronic intelligence should not be ignored, the key to success against terrorists is on the ground. This means training operators who know the language and the culture of the terrorists. Gaining these skills does indeed require the outlay of many 'ounces of silver'. It also requires time. The intelligence needs to be in place well before and well after the active campaign against the terrorists has started. As a back-up to one's own intelligence resources, the use of allied resources should be encouraged. Terrorist groups can, and more often than not do, operate across borders. Limiting intelligence resources to what is one's own is likely to limit what one can come to know, which in turn can lead to disaster.

Holding on to the moral high-ground

Although terrorists themselves are by nature stealthy, their campaigns of violence are largely public. Much of what they do is public relations. They use the mass media to claim credit for what they have done and thereby enhance the effect of their actions. They also use the mass media to communicate with their own people back home. In this part of their PR campaign, their aims are to look good in the eyes of their own people and to make their enemies look bad. When their enemies lapse into immorality, this amounts to the terrorists' enemies doing their PR work for them. Their enemies do this work free of charge. These lapses confirm their enemies' status as occupiers, exploiters, murderers and butchers, and confirm the status of the terrorists and their people as helpless and innocent victims.

For the enemies of terrorism, holding the moral high-ground is important for another reason. If these enemies are democratic states, they risk losing their own institutions if they act undemocratically. In time, the lapses make it less clear to their people what the difference is between the terrorists and their democratic enemies. When that happens, the democratic states will, sooner or later, lose the support of their people in their fight against terrorism. The lapses blur the difference between democratic states and terrorist groups, and so the people at home lose sight of what they are fighting for.

If, in spite of its efforts, a moral lapse occurs, the best damage-limitation policy is to deal with it promptly and openly. Damage will be unavoidable, but prompt action will, hopefully, keep it to manageable proportions. In part, what damage-control means is punishing the wrongdoers. Everyone knows that this is easier said than done. No institution enjoys dwelling on its mistakes. And we all know that it is difficult to apportion blame in the higher ranks of any institution. For that reason, some external review (even by members of allied forces) is required. There is no credibility in a review that regularly punishes only lower-ranked military and civilian personnel. And when no one is punished there is no credibility at all.

Alienating the terrorists from their constituency

Most commentators talk about separating the terrorists from their people. But how is this to be brought about when the terrorists work comfortably within their own culture and thus are able to shape what is said in their religious institutions, in their local newspapers, in schools, at market- and work-places, at social gatherings and in everyday conversations? Outsiders have an almost impossible task in trying to break into this web of connections. The best they can hope for is to bring about some alienation, but that is not easy. However, if the terrorists make mistakes such as punishing too many of their own people for not supporting them (see the Chechnya case-study in Chapter 4), becoming arrogant or lapsing into corruption, a counter-PR campaign led by the less radical members of the terrorists' community can gain some momentum. Outsider PR work might also help. But this kind of work is dangerous. If it becomes clear that outsiders are coordinating PR efforts with the less radical members, these members will lose credibility. So, outsider PR work needs to be very subtle.

Realistically, the best the enemies of terrorism can hope for is to keep from making matters worse. If the terrorists' enemies allow or encourage moral lapses among their military and government representatives (such as happened in Abu Ghraib prison during the Iraq War), catastrophe follows. This means that the bonding between the terrorists and their community becomes even tighter. Here talk about separation becomes simply laughable. The situation is so touchy that the outsiders may face difficulties even when they do not find themselves guilty of gross moral lapses. Consider how the thinking of the 'insiders' might go when the terrorists are backed into an urban setting by their militarily stronger opponent. Once the urban battle begins and casualties mount, how will these casualties be counted? Let us say that a hundred people are killed in a series of short encounters. As reported by the terrorists and their sympathizers, how many of the dead will be terrorists and how many will be innocent bystanders? It will not matter that 60 or so of the dead are in fact terrorists. Controlling as they do the means of communication within their own community, there will be nothing the outsiders can say or do to make the insiders believe otherwise. The following story shows how these matters work in the real world. An Iraqi friend of one of the authors reported a shooting incident (one of many) that took place in Mosul in 2004. She reported that, as usual, the Americans were not provoked in any way, and that their fire was totally indiscriminate. The Americans were reported to be shooting at everybody and everything. Our friend took what she reported as true without question even though she got the story from someone who got it from someone else.

Maintaining standards among civilian personnel

If private employers and employees are brought into the battle area, they should be held accountable to the same standards as are military personnel.[2] It makes no difference to the terrorists, their allies and sympathizers whether a moral lapse is committed by a soldier with a gun or a civilian with gun. The damage to the outsiders' campaign is the same. It is a catastrophe when soldiers misbehave, and it is a catastrophe when civilians do the same. Such lapses make it possible for the terrorists to criticize their opponents without having to go to the trouble of fabricating the truth – a practice that they are very good at.

Security as a priority

One of the few ways to separate or alienate terrorists from their constituency is protect the constituency from attack from all sides in the struggle. To do that, zones of security need to be established. These zones could be secured by domestic police and military forces supplemented by 'occupier' forces where necessary. The zones may be small at first, but can be expanded gradually. The idea of zones of security would probably work best in small and medium-sized communities. Judging by the Iraq experience, security is a crucial aspect of enabling a society to recover from a war. Without security (stability) nothing by way of reconstructing the infrastructure seems possible.

Jobs, Jobs, Jobs

Once there is even a modicum of security, the next step is to normalize people's lives by offering them opportunities to work. Ideally the jobs would be inside the security zone, as would be the residence of the workers. The employment programme would be closely tied to a strong PR programme that made it clear who is providing and guaranteeing the jobs. After all, the terrorists (e.g. Hamas) might be in the same line of work. It is incumbent upon the opponents of terrorism to tell the people involved that they are doing a better job of getting jobs for them than are the terrorists.

Heavy invasion; speedy withdrawal

It is important to send in a large invasion force, but to effect a withdrawal of 'occupying' forces as soon as possible. In retrospect, most agree that the size of the forces that invaded Iraq left too small a footprint. The coalition forces were more than adequate for defeating the Saddam regime, but not adequate for dealing with the aftermath of the war. The big-footprint style of fighting is not appropriate in some guerrilla/terrorist struggles. But when it is, a big rather than a small footprint is to be preferred so the job gets done quickly and efficiently. Forces with a big footprint crush the military forces supporting the terrorists quickly. But they also keep insurgencies from maturing into powerful guerrilla forces. Since military police know how to maintain law and order better than regular military forces, the big-footprint forces need to be well represented by police.

Small forces create another problem. As they tend to drag matters out, they leave plenty of time for the people to develop a genuine hatred of the 'occupiers' – even if they are doing an efficient job and, generally speaking, keeping their hands clean. This 'quick in-and-out' policy fits in well with the policy (articulated above) of identifying one's enemy and goals. Both policies emphasize placing limits on military ventures. These ventures should not aim to change the nature of the world (or humanity). Rather, they should aim to do specific jobs that are doable. Once these jobs are done, the outside forces should retreat to remote but nearby corners of the area of battle and then leave the settling of political battles to the locals. The results may not always be to the liking of the occupiers, but even that is likely to be a better outcome than becoming embroiled in an endless struggle.

Non-military (external) recommendations

Diplomacy

Diplomacy should be used wherever possible. If, however, diplomatic moves are made with nations that have some sort of sympathy with the terrorists, one should not be hopeful about the results that might be achieved. Nonetheless, given the high cost of going to war, diplomacy should always be a first resort.

Cooperation

Cooperation with allies is crucial in the pursuit of terrorists. Terrorists can move easily across borders, both physically and electronically. Mobility is one of the features of the 'new terrorism' that makes it new (see Chapter 4). If they are pressured in one country, terrorists can easily move to another to do their work in relative safety. As they move across borders, so must those who are chasing them. But this cross-border pursuit can only be accomplished when those nations on the 'other side' cooperate. Of course, these other nations may not be willing to cooperate, or they may do so in a way that is not ideal. However, some cooperation is generally better than none in tracking down terrorists or gaining useful intelligence about them and certainly better than 'going it alone'.

Employment

We discussed employment, in the previous section, in the context of an improving war situation. But jobs are also important in peacetime. They are important not only because they generate money to help people support their families but also because of what they produce. Jobs that help construct highways, bridges, schools, hospitals, etc. make life better for a population and thus tempts them not to engage in revolt and terrorism.[3] If, after a period of relative quiet, unemployment begins to rise again, trouble should be expected.

Terrorists and other insurgents have a habit of returning to the scenes of their old crimes. To keep them at bay, job-creation policies have to be continually renewed.

Non-military (internal) recommendations

Security

Airports, key government buildings and the like need continued protection. They are so vulnerable to attack that security needs to be maintained. But security for maritime docking facilities, chemical plants, power stations, bridges, etc. needs to be upgraded. The upgrading should be reasonable rather than absolute. No nation can afford a blanket of protection for all major facilities, and for the people who work in them. So, all nations should realize that if a major terrorist event occurs within its borders, it may be that no one is to blame for it happening.

Educating the public

The terrorizing effect of terrorism is only partly due to the act of terrorism itself. If the act is particularly cruel and large-scale it will have a considerable impact. But the impact will be magnified if the act is repeatedly shown on television and commented on by government officials in a dramatic and panicky way. In magnifying the effect of the terrorist act, television and the government are effectively working hand-in-glove with the terrorists. There is a better way of reacting. The media, especially television, can do more than show vivid pictures of catastrophes: they can also give extensive background information about how, for example, deaths due to terrorism with deaths due to other causes. They can also emphasize how we play into the hands of terrorists by allowing ourselves to become panic-stricken, and how and why it is that some people are more likely to panic as a result of a terrorist attack. In short, television (and again the other mass media) can play an educative role.

Similarly, politicians, especially national leaders, need to educate the public concerning the remoteness and nearness of terrorism, so that they may be better prepared for the next attack.

This calmer response should eventually have an effect on the terrorists. If they see that they are not having a great effect on a population, they will respond in one of two ways. The first is that they may escalate their attacks. They will use bigger bombs, employ more suicide bombers and/or engage in grosser forms of terrorism (e.g. torturing victims before killing them) until they get the kind of response they desire. There is a real possibility that this is how they will respond, and a nation must be aware of this. But escalation is not easy, and terrorists may not have the resources or skills to go down that road. The second way of responding to a non-terrorized opponent is for terrorists to give up – either gradually or suddenly.

Thus although there is a danger in educating the public about terrorism, there may be a greater danger in not educating them and thus leaving them in a mental state in which they can be easily manipulated by terrorists. Educating the population would seem to be a risk worth taking.

Forecasting worst-case scenarios

Terrorism today is not hugely destructive in terms of injury or loss of life. More people die or are injured in road accidents than by acts of terrorism. As Richardson put it: 'The probability that terrorists will kill as many Americans as drunk drivers in any given years is tiny.'[4] Terrorism just seems more destructive because of its (planned) dramatic effect. If people educate themselves not to overreact to present-day terrorism, they should be able to live with it.

What should be feared more is tomorrow's terrorism. Richardson again:

The only way that terrorists could inflict real and lasting damage on us is if they were to acquire a weapon of mass destruction, and not just any weapon of mass destruction. A dirty bomb or a chemical weapon could inflict serious damage but pose no real threat. The one way they could truly harm us is if they were to acquire and deploy a biological or nuclear weapon.[5]

It is escalated terrorism that should worry us most and so should receive increased attention via a more systematic monitoring of nuclear weapons sites and materials.

Reducing reliance on oil

Many present-day terrorists are funded by oil money. This money gets into the pockets of terrorists because nations such as Saudi Arabia, Iran and Sudan are experiencing good times. The price of oil is high. Some of the extra money made by these countries, and by the oil barons from these countries, gets passed on to one terrorist group or another. According to Thomas Friedman,[6] some of this money supports, even props up, those oil-producing nations that support terrorism:

In 2005, Bloomberg.com reported Iran's government earned $44.6 billion from oil and spent $25 billion on subsidies – for housing, jobs, food and 34-cents-a-gallon gasoline – to buy off interest groups. Iran's current populist president has further increased the goods and services being subsidized.

So if oil prices fall sharply again, Iran's regime will have to take away many benefits from many Iranians, as the Soviets had to do. For a regime already unpopular with many of its people, that could cause all kinds of problems ...

In short, the best tool we have for curbing Iran's influence is not containment or engagement, but getting the price of oil down in the long term with conservation and an alternative energy strategy. Let's exploit Iran's oil addiction by ending ours.[7]

So cutting down on oil use means that the pockets of those who support terrorists will not be so heavy with dollars and euros as they are now. That, in turn, should harm the terrorist cause since their pockets will be lighter as well. They will no longer be in a position to aid other terrorists as, for example, the terrorists in Chechnya were in the late 1990s.

Afterthoughts

Terrorism has changed. Corresponding to the two major forms of terrorism, it has changed in two ways. First, in all or almost all wars, *state* terrorism is obsolete. It is no longer possible for states with democratic pretensions to practise terrorism aimed at innocent populations. Apart from being disinclined to use this form of terrorism as something incompatible with democratic societies, they have two concrete reasons for not practising terrorism any longer. The first has to do with military technology. As against those days in the Second World War when weapons (especially bombs and shells) were unsophisticated (see Chapter 3 for the case of the British bombing of Germany), today's weapons are capable of precise targeting. Major democratic military powers have by now developed and deployed a wide variety of sophisticated weaponry. And they continue to develop still more.[8] All this makes it possible for them to fight wars that track the principle of discrimination in a way that was inconceivable two or three decades ago. With smart weapons in hand, the moral pressure to use them, rather than 'dumb' bombs, increases.

The second major factor moving democratic nations away from employing terrorism against innocent populations is the video camera. The camera makes it impossible for these nations to mount dirty campaigns. It would not take long for the camera to uncover what was going on and expose the 'crime'. In short order, the disgraced government would find itself under great political pressure to stop what it was doing. It might even find itself thrown out of office.

The second way that terrorism has changed has to do with non-state terrorism. In contrast to the obsolete status of state terrorism, non-state terrorism is thriving. The very mass media technologies that constrain states from engaging in terrorism are what help non-state terrorists make their form of work better today than it was in the past. The media act as terror multipliers. In so acting, they ensure that the terrorists get the maximum benefit from their horrible deeds. Without the media, an act of terror terrorizes locally. With the media, it terrorizes internationally. Without the media, some friends of the terrorists hear of their deeds and feel proud of what their brave freedom-fighters have done. With the media, all their friends, worldwide, hear what was done and are proud.

It is not likely that the effects of the media in enhancing terrorism will change in the future. These effects may in fact increase. As more people gain access to television and computers, so more of them will be influenced by what they see and hear electronically.

Military technology has the opposite effect on state and non-state actors, just as the electronic media do. As we have noted, technology in the form of sophisticated weaponry discourages states from engaging in terrorism. But military technology encourages non-state actors. Smaller but more powerful bombs make it possible for terrorists to get a better return on their violent efforts. They can kill and maim more people, and they can terrorize more people as well.

We have argued that other factors besides the media and military technology contribute to the flourishing of terrorism. However, most of these factors (e.g. injustice) have always been around and so have always encouraged the few to engage in terrorist acts and campaigns. What makes terrorism new in this century and late in the previous one are the media and military technology. They are the causes of terrorism that ensure that for the foreseeable future we will indeed be living in a new world disorder.

Notes

Chapter 1

1. Walter Laqueur, *The New Terrorism: Fanaticism and the Arms of Mass Destruction* (New York and Oxford: Oxford University Press, 1999), p. 5.
2. Ibid., p. 8.
3. Tony Coady, 'Defining Terrorism', in *Terrorism: The Philosophical Issues*, ed. Igor Primoratz (New York: Palgrave Macmillan, 2004), p. 3.
4. Michael Walzer, *Just and Unjust Wars: A Moral Argument with Historical Illustrations* (New York: Basic Books, 1977), pp. 197–206. See also Coady 'Defining Terrorism'.
5. Strictly speaking, the claim that terrorism contrasts with other tactics such as blockades and envelopment must be qualified. Although still a tactic, terrorism depends on other tactics for its implementation. The nature of this dependence will become evident in later chapters.
6. Nick Fotion, Bruno Coppieters and Ruben Apressyan, Introduction to *Moral Constraints on War: Principles and Cases*, ed. Bruno Coppieters and Nick Fotion (New York: Lexington, 2002), pp. 11–15.

Chapter 2

1. *Wikipedia*, 'Assassins', http://www/skewme.com/assassin.html, accessed 14 November 2006.
2. Hugh Barlow, *Dead for Good: Martyrdom and the Rise of the Suicide Bomber* (Boulder, CO: Paradigm, 2007), pp. 74–8.

3. Mia Bloom, *Dying to Kill: The Allure of Suicide Terror* (New York: Columbia University Press, 2005), p. 76.

4. In personal communication, an Iraqi woman said that her father, a soldier in the Iraqi army, was *martyred* in the Iraq/Iran war of the 1980s. It was not clear whether she was speaking metaphorically or literally.

5. Liberation Tigers of Tamil Eelam.

6. Babbar Khalsa International. The goal of this group is to achieve Sikh independence in Punjab.

7. Kurdistan Workers' Party.

8. Robert A. Pape, *Dying to Win: The Strategic Logic of Suicide Terrorism* (New York: Random House, 2005), pp. 64–5.

9. Christian Caryl, 'Why they do it', *New York Review of Books*, 22 September 2005.

Chapter 3

1. A. Geifman, *Thou Shalt Kill. Revolutionary Terrorism in Russia, 1894–1917* (Princeton, NJ: Princeton University Press, 1993), p. 3.

2. V. Malinin, *Istoriya Russkogo Utopicheskogo Sotsialisma. Vtoraya polovina 19 – nachalo 20 vv* (Moscow: Nauka, 1991), p. 66.

3. The noted terrorist Ivan Kaliaev once refused to toss a bomb into the Grand Duke's carriage as soon as he learned that the Grand Duke's family was accompanying him.

4. Geifman, *Thou Shalt Kill*, p. 21.

5. The sense of a mission was always strong among the Jews. In this regard Marx was called by Russian philosopher N. Berdyaev, 'a very typical Jew'.

6. Geifman, *Thou Shalt Kill*, p. 40.

7. Sergei Nechaev (1848–83) was one of the most notorious terrorists of the older generation. He murdered one of his own men – a student by the name of Ivanov – who questioned the authority of his leader. Later, Nechaev was arrested by the government on the charge of murder. Nechaev never hesitated to use force and fraud even towards his followers in order to achieve strict compliance and to get money. His behaviour was generally regarded by the revolutionaries of the first wave as immoral. Dostoevsky depicted Nechaev in his

novel *The Devils* (1872), which was also the name he gave to terrorists in general.

8. The Devil is supposed to ride a pale horse at the end of time.
9. Hugh Strachan, *The First World War* (London: Penguin, 2005), p. 203.
10. Ibid., pp. 210–14.
11. John Keegan, *The First World War* (New York: Alfred A. Knopf, 1999), pp. 273–4.
12. Strachan, *The First World War*, p. 215.
13. Ibid., p. 215.
14. Keegan, *The First World War*, p. 353.
15. A.J.P. Taylor, *A History of the First World War* (New York: Berkley, 1966), pp. 114–15. See also Keegan, *The First World War*, pp. 353–4.
16. Ibid., p. 115.
17. Ibid., p. 114.
18. B.H. Liddell Hart, *History of the Second World War* (New York: Putnam's, 1970), pp. 589–93.
19. D.B. Tubbs, *Lancaster Bomber* (New York: Ballantine Books, 1972), p. 11.
20. Liddell Hart, *History of the Second World War*, p. 595.
21. Noble Franklin, *Bomber Offensive: The Devastation of Europe* (New York: Ballantine Books, 1970), pp. 41, 55–6.
22. Liddell Hart, *History of the Second World War*, p. 593.
23. Stephen A. Garrett, 'Terror Bombing of German Cities in World War II', in *Terrorism: The Philosophical Issues*, ed. Igor Primoratz (London: Palgrave/ Macmillan, 2004), pp. 141–2.
24. A storm (a divine wind) in 1281 destroyed Kublai Khan's large fleet in its attempt to invade Japan.
25. A.J. Barker, *Suicide Weapon* (New York: Ballantine Books, 1971), p. 75.
26. I.C.B. Dear (ed.), *The Oxford Companion to World War II* (Oxford: Oxford University Press, 1995), p. 101.
27. Ibid., p. 318.
28. Ibid., p. 836.
29. Robert A. Pape, *Dying to Win: The Strategic Logic of Suicide Terrorism* (New York: Random House, 2005), pp. 35–7.
30. Louise Richardson, *What Terrorists Want* (New York: Random House, 2006), pp. 89–91.

31. Walter Laqueur, *The New Terrorism: Fanaticism and the Arms of Mass Destruction* (New York and Oxford: Oxford University Press, 1999), p. 33.

32. Wikipedia, 'Provisional Irish Republican Army', http://www.answers.com/topic/provisional-irish-republican-army, accessed 24 October 2006.

33. Ibid.

34. Ibid.

35. Caleb Carr, *The Lessons of Terror* (New York: Random House, 2002), p. 206.

36. *Wikipedia*, 'Provisional Irish Republican Army'.

37. 'Aceh', http://en.wikipedia.org/wiki/Aceh, accessed June 2006.

38. Lea E. Williams, *Southeast Asia: A History* (Oxford: Oxford University Press, 1976), p. 133.

39. Peter Hamburger, 'Song of the Holy War', *Quarterly Journal of Military History*, 18.4 (summer 2006): 33.

40. Ibid., p. 35.

41. Ibid., p. 40–1.

42. MIPT Terrorism Knowledge Base, 'Free Aceh Movement (GAM)', http://www.tkb.org/Group.jsp?groupID=3600, 10 May 2006, accessed 4 June 2006.

43. Hamid Papang, 'Massacre of Muslims in Aceh–Sumatra revives calls for independence', http://www.muslimedia.com/archives/sea99/aceh-kill.htm, 16–31 May 1999, accessed 4 June 2006.

44. Solonas Gregoriadis, *A History of Dictatorship* (Athens: Kapopoulos, 1975), pp. 289–300.

45. M. Bossis, *Greece and Terrorism. National and International Dimensions* (Athens–Komotini: Sakoulas, 1996), p. 120.

46. Proclamation published in *Eleftherotypia*, April 1977.

47. Martha Crenshaw, 'An organizational approach to the analysis of political terrorism', *Orbis*, 29.3 (1985): 466.

48. Alexis Papaxelas and Tasos Telloglou, *17th November Investigation* (Athens: Estia, 2003), p. 79.

49. Georgios Karampelas, *Greek City Partisans, 1974–1985* (Athens: Grafes, 2002), pp. 33–4. The relevant proclamation of the organization is also in the *Eleftherotypia* and *Nea* papers of late December 1976.

50. 17 November, *The Proclamations* (Athens: Cactos, 2002), p. 304.

51. Proclamation published in *Ethnos*, 11 November 1988.

52. Papaxelas and Telloglou, *17th November Investigation*, pp. 167–8.

53. Ibid., pp. 195–261.

Chapter 4

1. Walter Laqueur, *The New Terrorism: Fanaticism and the Arms of Mass Destruction* (New York and Oxford: Oxford University Press, 1999), pp. 191–6.

2. http://en.wikipedia.org/wiki/Ethnic_conflict_in_Sri_Lanka, accessed 23 June 2006.

3. Robert Pape, *Dying to Win: The Strategic Logic of Suicide Terrorism* (New York: Random House, 2005), p. 141.

4. Hugh Barlow, *Dead for Good: Martydom and the Rise of Suicide Bombers* (Boulder, CO: Paradigm, 2007), p. 134.

5. Pape, *Dying to Win*, p. 227. See also Rajeev Sharma, *Beyond the Tigers: Tracking Rajiv Gandhi's Assassination* (New Delhi: Kaveri Books, 1998), pp. 44–6.

6. Joseph Brewda and Madhu Gurung, 'Southern India, Sri Lanka terrorist groups', *Executive Intelligence Review*, 13 October 1995.

7. Ibid.

8. Basayev lost almost all his relatives in the Russian indiscriminate aviation attack on Vedeno village. One may claim that the first terrorist operation of the Russian–Chechen war was provoked by revenge.

9. Valery Tishkov, *Chechnya: Life in a War-Torn Society* (Berkeley, CA: University of California Press, 2004), p. 201.

10. One of the major Chechen religious leaders, Akhmad Kadyrov, said: 'The Chechens did not become Russians in 300 years of occupation and they are not going to become Arabs as well.'

11. We won't just sit here in Chechnya and be exterminated. I warned that we would fight in Russia and there are a lot more targets. We have radioactive elements, biological weapons that Russia left us. We could put biological weapons in Yekaterinburg and let them all get sick. To put uranium in Moscow would require one person. One of our people gets killed and a city dies with him … If someone spits at you in the face for half a year, wouldn't you spit back just once? That's what we did and we'll do it again.
   Interview with Shamil Basayev, in Sebastian Smith, *Allah's Mountains: The Battle for Chechnya* (London: Tauris, 2001), p. 200.

12. V.N. Krasnov, 'Approaches to the study of suicide terrorism', in *Psychological Responses to the New Terrorism – A NATO–Russian Dialogue*, ed. S. Wessely (Amsterdam: IOS Press, 2005), p. 108.

13. On 10 November 1975 the UN General Assembly adopted a resolution defining Zionism as 'a form of racism and racial discrimination'.

14. According to Robespierre, 'Terror is a consequence of the general principle of democracy applied to the most pressing needs of the fatherland.'

15. 'I will send forth My terror before you, and I will throw into panic all the people among whom you come, and I will make all your enemies turn tail before you … I will drive them out before you little by little, until you have increased and possessed the land' (Exodus 23.27).

16. Ahron Bregman, *Israel's Wars, 1947–1993* (Florence, KY: Routledge, 2000), p. 13.

17. On 2 November 1917, in a letter from Lord Balfour to Lord Rothschild, the British notified the Zionists that the proposal to found an independent Jewish state in Palestine was acceptable. The British promise to the Jews of a 'national home' in Palestine was turned into an international commitment when the League of Nations, on 24 July 1922, reiterated the British pledge in a document which assigned a mandate of Palestine to Britain.

18. Bregman, *Israel's Wars*, p. 11.

19. Thomas G. Mitchell, *Native vs. Settler: Ethnic Conflict in Israel/Palestine, Northern Ireland and South Africa* (Westport, CT: Greenwood, 2000), p. 131.

20. Bregman, *Israel's Wars*, p. 33.

21. Israel was forced to wage this war. Unlike Egypt and other Arab states, Israel had to mobilize all its reserve troops in the face of an inevitable strike and could not continue postponing its military actions indefinitely without seriously jeopardizing its chances of defence.

22. In November 1974, in his address to the UN General Assembly, Arafat clarified his understanding of terrorism: 'The only description for these acts is that they are acts of barbarism … And yet, the Zionist racists and colonialists have the temerity to describe the just struggle of our people as terror. Could there be a more flagrant distortion of the truth than this?'

23. The Israeli secret service.

24. Mitchell, *Native vs. Settler*, pp. 52–3.

25. Even after becoming civilians, the Israelis, as Chief of Staff Yadin once put it, remain 'soldiers on eleven months' annual leave'. In other words the IDF is the people of Israel in uniform and the people of Israel are the IDF without uniform.

26. Mitchell Geoffrey Bard, *Complete Idiot's Guide to the Middle East Conflict.* (Indianapolis, IN: Alpha Books, 1999), p. 379.

27. Farhad Khosrokhavar, *Suicide Bombers. Allah's New Martyrs* (London and Ann Arbor, MI: Pluto Press, 2005), p. 112.

28. Jeffrey Gettleman, 'War in Sudan? Not where the oil wealth flows', *New York Times*, 24 October 2006.

29. Nicholas D. Kristof, 'Genocide slow motion', *New York Review of Books*, 9 (February 2006): 14.

30. Julie Flint and Alex de Waal, *Darfur: A Short History of a Long* War (London and New York: Zed Books, 2005), p. 102.

31. Gerard Prunier, *Darfur: The Ambiguous Genocide* (Ithaca, NY: Cornell University Press, 2005), pp. 148–58. Prunier has an excellent discussion as to why it is difficult to confirm casualty figures in Darfur.

32. Flint and de Waal, *Darfur*, pp. 109–10.

33. Ibid., pp. 105–6.

34. Khosrokhavar, *Suicide Bombers*, p. 162.

35. The historical Caliphate was abolished by Kemal Ataturk in 1924.

36. Sacred religious war of Islam waged on unbelievers.

37. Many *surahs* of the Koran sound like a guidance for contemporary Islamic terrorists. For example: 'But those who did wrong changed the world from that had been told to them for another, so We sent upon the wrong-doers a punishment from the heaven because of their rebelling against Allah's obedience' (Koran. *Surah* 2. Al-Baqarah (59).

38. One of the most militant groups is Al-Muhjiroun. It wants to turn Britain into an Islamic country.

39. John Keegan, *The Iraq War* (New York: Vintage Books/Random House, 2004, 2005), pp. 137–8.

40. Ibid., p. 204.

41. Michael R. Gordon and Bernard E. Trainor, 'Dash to Baghdad left top US generals dividied', *New York Times*, 13 March 2006.

42. Keegan, *The Iraq War*, p. 207.

43. Marc Santora 'One year later, Golden Mosque is still in ruins', *New York Times*, 13 February 2007.

44. Damien Cave and Ahmad Fadam, 'Iraq insurgents employ chlorine in bomb attacks', *New York Times*, 22 February 2007.

45. Nina Kamp, Michael O'Hanlon, Amy Unikewicz, 'The state of Iraq: an update', *New York Times*, 16 June 2006.

Chapter 5

1. Stephen A. Garrett, 'Terror Bombing of German Cities in World War II', in *Terrorism: The Philosophical Issues*, ed. Igor Primoratz (London: Palgrave/Macmillan, 2004), p. 151.
2. B.H. Liddell Hart, *History of the Second World War* (New York: Putnam's, 1970), pp. 589–90.
3. A.N. Frankland, 'Strategic Air Offensives', in *Oxford Companion to World War II*, ed. I.C.B. Dear and M.R.D. Foot (Oxford: Oxford University Press, 1995), pp. 1070–71.
4. Hugh Strachan, *The First World War* (London: Penguin, 2003), p. 99.
5. John Keegan, *The First World War* (New York: Alfred A. Knopf, 1999), p. 223.
6. Strachan, *The First World War*, pp. 111–12.
7. Yehuda Bauer, *A History of the Holocaust* (New York: Franklin Watts, 1982), p. 99.
8. Ibid., p. 100.
9. Ibid., p. 107.
10. Robert A. Pape, *Dying to Win* (New York: Random House, 2005), pp. 80–81.
11. Ibid., p. 100.
12. Ibid., p. 94.
13. Hezbollah, 'Program (February 1985)', in *Anti-American Terrorism and the Middle East*, ed. Barry Rubin and Judith Colp Rubin (Oxford: Oxford University Press, 2002), pp. 50–54. (See also p. 36.)
14. Farhad Khosrokhavar, *Suicide Bombers: Allah's New Martyrs* (London and Ann Arbor, MI: Pluto Press, 2005), p. 48.

Chapter 6

1. Anne Marie Oliver and Paul Steinberg, *The Road to Martyrs' Square: A Journey into the World of the Suicide Bomber* (Oxford and New York: Oxford University Press, 2005), p. 60.
2. Robert A. Pape, *Dying to Win: The Strategic Logic of Suicide Terrorism* (New York, Random House, 2005), p. 226.

3. Mia Bloom, *Dying to Kill: The Allure of Suicide Terror* (New York: Columbia University Press, 2005), pp. 159–60.

4. Louise Richardson, *What Terrorists Want* (New York: Random House, 2006), p. 42.

5. Ibid., p. 128.

6. Ibid., p. 41.

7. Ibid., p. 5.

8. Gordon A. Craig, *Germany: 1866–1945* (Oxford and New York: Oxford University Press, 1978), pp. 597–601.

9. Peter H. Merkl, *The Making of a Stormtrooper* (Princeton, NJ: Princeton University Press, 1980), pp. 283–308.

10. Bloom, *Dying to Kill*, p. 87.

11. Richardson, *What Terrorists Want*, p. 117.

12. Bloom, *Dying to Kill*, pp. 86–8.

13. Richardson, *What Terrorists Want*, p. 126.

14. Ibid., p. 126.

15. Ibid., p. 127.

Chapter 7

1. David Zeidan, 'The Islamist View of Life as a Perennial Battle', in *Anti-American Terrorism and the Middle East*, ed. Barry Rubin and Judith Colp Rubin (Oxford and New York: Oxford University Press, 2002), pp. 11–27. See also Ayman Al-Zawahiri, 'Why Attack America (January 2002)', ibid., p. 132.

2. Richard Scott, 'Scourge of the seas', *Jane's Defence Weekly*, 1 May 2005: 20–23.

3. Carlotta Gall, 'Despite years of US pressure, Taliban fight on in jagged hills', *New York Times*, 4 June 2005.

4. David Kocieniewski, 'Rows of loosely guarded targets lie just outside New York City', *New York Times*, 9 May 2005.

5. Editorial, 'Chemical time bombs', *New York Times*, 10 May 2005.

6. John Tierney, 'Bombs bursting on air', *New York Times*, 10 May 2005.

7. Once again, our broad characterization of terrorism contrasts with narrower characterizations found in many writings on this subject. See,

for example, articles by Igor Primoratz ('What is Terrorism?') and Tony Coady ('Defining Terrorism') in *Terrorism: The Philosophical Issues*, ed. Igor Primoratz (New York: Palgrave/Macmillan, 2004), pp. 15–27 and pp. 3–14 respectively. See also David Rodin 'Terrorism without intention', in *Ethics*, July 2004: 751–71and Ninian Stephen, 'Toward a Definition of Terrorism', in *Terrorism and Justice*, ed. Tony Coady and Michael O'Keefe (Victoria: Melbourne University Press, 2002), pp. 1–7. See also Title 22 of the US Code, Section 2656 f(d). All of these references restrict the meaning of 'terrorism' to attacks on innocents, civilians, non-combatants, the defenceless, etc. Our view has been (see Chapter 1) that central to the meaning of terrorism is that it is a tactic of war or violent struggle that can be used against non-combatants *and* others as well. On our account it is possible, for example, for terrorists to victimize military personnel in part in order to terrorize others such as non-combatants and government officials. It is also possible for terrorists to attack half-trained military personnel in order to panic them into deserting. Thus, anybody can be victimized, not just innocents, in order to trigger terror in others; or for that matter anybody can be terrorized in order to be victimized (e.g. as when soldiers are terrorized by a screaming siren and in their terror become more vulnerable to attack). On this view, individuals or groups become terrorists when their main tactic is terrorism. Of course, they are terrorists when they actually succeed in terrorizing. But, in an extended sense of 'terrorist', they are terrorists even when their serious attempts at terrorizing others fail. 'Terrorist' and 'terrorism' are not success words in the way that 'murderer' and 'murder' are. A murderer is a murderer only if he or she succeeds in murdering. An attempted murder is not a kind of murder. But a terrorist is a terrorist even if his or her attempt fails. So the terror concepts as a family word more like 'aggressor' and 'aggression'. An aggressor is an aggressor even if his or her aggression is deflected. A further (but small) extension of the meaning of 'terrorist' allows for one who does not intend to terrorize but in fact does to be counted as a terrorist. One other point about the terror concepts needs to be made. Terrorists can also be guerrillas. The two concepts do not exclude each other. As a result one is not forced to say something like 'Since these fighters killed military personnel today, and sent their comrades into a state of terror, they cannot be terrorists but, rather, are guerrilla fighters.' But it makes little difference whether one accepts our broader sense of the terror concepts or not. Most of the points made about persistence apply to both to the broad and to the narrow sense of terrorism.

8. John Kerry is quoted by Jeffrey Goldberg ('The unbranding: can Democrats make themselves look tough', *New Yorker*, 21 March 2005: 34) as follows:

> The bottom line is that, if you look at the data, the appearance of the Osama Bin Laden tape [late in October of 2004] had a profound impact [on the election]. The fact is that we flatlined on that day. I presented stronger arguments, but there was a visceral unwillingness to change Commander-in-Chief five days after the Bin Laden tape.

9. Abu Ubeid Al-Qurashi, 'September 11 as a Great Success' in Rubin and Colp (eds), *Anti-American Terrorism and the Middle East*:

> [As a result of the Munich attack] thousands of young Palestinians were roused to join the *fedayeen* organizations … The number of organizations engaging in international 'terror' increased from a mere eleven in 1968 to fifty-five in 1978. Fifty-four percent of these new organizations sought to imitate the success of the Palestinian organizations – particularly the publicity of Palestinian cause garnered after Munich. (p. 275)

10. Carlotta Gall, 'Afghan fight ends in death of 20 rebels', *New York Times*, 20 June 2005. Supposedly the Taliban were defeated in the war of 2002. But as guerrillas and/or terrorists they keep coming back. Gall tells of attacks on police stations and the capture of 11 policemen. She also tells of the killing of a judge and two other government officials in ambush. She then closes her article as follows:

> The killings [by the Taliban] are among a series of assaults in the south and east of the country in recent weeks – including a deadly attack on a team of doctors, a tribal elder and an election worker – that the Afghan authorities and American military have said are part of a new campaign by the Taliban and other insurgents intent on disrupting parliamentary elections in September.

See also Carlotta Gall, 'Taliban rebels still menacing Afghan south', *New York Times*, 2 March 2006.

11. Michael Specter, 'Kremlin, inc.', *The New Yorker*, 29 January 2007: 50–63.

Chapter 8

1. Hamas, 'Charter (August 1988)', in *Anti-American Terrorism and the Middle East: A Documentary Reader*, ed. Barry Rubin and Judith Colp Rubin (Oxford and New York: Oxford University Press, 2002), p. 56.
2. Hezbollah, 'Program (February 1985)', ibid., p. 51.
3. Osama Bin Laden, 'Declaration of War (August 1996)', ibid., p. 137.
4. Hezbollah 'Program', p. 53.
5. Joseph Lelyveld, 'Jimmy Carter and apartheid', *New York Review of Books*, 29 March 2007: 14–17.
6. Hamas 'Charter', p. 55.
7. Ayman Al-Zawahiri, 'Why Attack America (January 2002)', in Rubin and Rubin (eds), *Anti-American, Terrorism*, p. 132.
8. The Palestine Information Centre, 'Hamas: Israel to shoulder responsibility for end of calm', 27 December 2006, http://www.palestine-info.co.uk/am/publish/article_21019.shtml, accessed 27 June 2006.
9. Al-Zawahiri, 'Why Attack America', p. 133.
10. John Ray Skates, *The Invasion of Japan: Alternative to the Bomb* (Columbia, SC: University of South Carolina Press, 1994), p. 256. Casualty estimates concerning the invasion of the island of Kyushu (operation OLYMPIC) vary wildly. Skates reckons that American casualties would have been comparable to those at Okinawa. Thus the Americans, he says, could have expected to suffer between 60,000–70,000 casualties. Of these, the dead would total some 15,000–20,000. Japanese casualties he assesses at well over 250,000. These estimates are conservative compared with those of some other writers.

Chapter 9

1. Sheikh Muhammad Sayyed Tantawi, 'Suicide Operations are Legitimate Defense (8 April 1997)', in *Anti-American Terrorism and the Middle East*, ed. Barry Rubin and Judith Colp Rubin (Oxford and New York: Oxford University Press, 2002), p. 36.
2. World Islamic Front, 'Statement: Jihad against Jews and Crusaders (23 February 1998', ibid., pp. 149–50.

3. R.M. Hare, *Moral Thinking: Its Levels, Method and Point* (Oxford: Clarendon Press, 1981). See Chs 5 and 6.

4. Michael Walzer, *Just and Unjust Wars* (New York: Basic Books, 1977), pp. 251–68.

5. Robert A. Pape, *Dying to Win: The Strategic Logic of Suicide Terrorism* (New York: Random House, 2005), p. 40.

Chapter 10

1. Sun Tzu, *The Art of War*, ed. James Clavell (New York: Dell, 1983), p. 77.

2. T. Christian Miller, *Blood Money: Wasted Billions, Lost Lives, and Corporate Greed in Iraq* (New York: Little, Brown, 2006).

3. Nicholas D. Kristof, 'Aid workers with guns', *New York Times*, 4 March 2007.

4. Louise Richardson, *What Terrorists Want* (New York: Random House, 2006), p. 232.

5. Ibid., p. 233.

6. Thomas L. Friedman, 'The oil-addicted ayatollahs', *New York Times*, 2 February 2007.

7. Ibid.

8. Amy Butler, 'Sharpening focus: USAF testing continues on variant of small-diameter bomb', *Aviation Week and Space Technology*, 26 February 2007: 28. The bomb is designed to keep collateral damage to a minimum (especially in urban settings).

Bibliography

Al-Qurashi, Abu Ubeid, 'September 11 as a Great Success (27 February 2002)', in *Anti-American Terrorism and the Middle East*, ed. Barry Rubin and Judith Colp Rubin (Oxford and New York: Oxford University Press, 2002).

Al-Zawahiri, 'Why Attack America (January 2002)', in *Anti-American Terrorism and the Middle East*, ed. Barry Rubin and Judith Colp Rubin (Oxford and New York: Oxford University Press, 2002).

Bard, Mitchell Geoffrey, *Complete Idiot's Guide to the Middle East Conflict* (Indianapolis, IN: Alpha Books, 1999).

Barker, A.J., *Suicide Weapon* (New York: Ballantine Books, 1971).

Barlow, Hugh, *Dead for Good: Martyrdom and the Rise of the Suicide Bomber* (Boulder, CO: Paradigm, 2007).

Bauer, Yehuda, *A History of the Holocaust* (New York: Franklin Watts, 1982).

Bin Laden, Osama, 'Declaration of War (August 1996)', in *Anti-American Terrorism and the Middle East*, ed. Barry Rubin and Judith Colp Rubin (Oxford and New York: Oxford University Press, 2002).

Bloom, Mia, *Dying to Kill: The Allure of Suicide Terror* (New York: Columbia University Press, 2005).

Bossis, M., *Greece and Terrorism: National and International Dimensions* (Athens–Komotini: Sakoulas, 1996).

Bregman, Ahron, *Israel's Wars, 1947–1993* (Florence, KY: Routledge, 2000).

Brewda, Joseph and Gurung, Madhu, 'Southern India, Sri Lanka terrorist groups', *Executive Intelligence Review*, 13 October 1995.

Butler, Amy, 'Sharpening focus: USAF testing continues on variant of small-diameter bomb', *Aviation Week and Space Technology*, 26 February 2007.

Carr, Caleb, *The Lessons of Terror* (New York: Random House, 2002).

Caryl, Christian, 'Why they do it', *New York Review of Books*, 22 September 2005.

Cave, Damien and Fadam, Ahmad, 'Iraq insurgents employ chlorine in bomb attacks', *New York Times*, 22 February 2007.

Coady, Tony, 'Defining Terrorism', in *Terrorism: The Philosophical Issues*, ed. Igor Primoratz (New York: Palgrave Macmillan, 2004).

Craig, Gordon A., *Germany: 1866–1945* (Oxford and New York: Oxford University Press, 1978).

Crenshaw, Martha, 'An organizational approach to the analysis of political terrorism,' *Orbis*, 29.3 (1985).

Dear, I.C.B. and M.R.D. Foot (eds), *Oxford Companion to World War II* (Oxford and New York: Oxford University Press, 1996).

Flint, Julie and de Waal, Alex, *Darfur: A Short History of a Long War* (London and New York: Zed Books, 2005).

Fotion, Nick, Coppieters, Bruno and Apressyan, Ruben, 'Introduction', in *Moral Constraints on War: Principles and Cases*, ed. Bruno Coppieters and Nick Fotion (New York: Lexington, 2002).

Frankland, A.N., 'Strategic Air Offensives', in *Oxford Companion to World War II*, ed. I.C.B. Dear and M.R.D. Foot (Oxford: Oxford University Press, 1996).

Franklin, Noble, *Bomber Offensive: The Devastation of Europe* (New York: Ballantine Books, 1970).

Friedman, Thomas L., 'The oil-rich ayatollahs', *New York Times*, 2 February 2007.

Gall, Carlotta, 'Despite years of US pressure, Taliban fight on in jagged hills', *New York Times*, 4 June 2005.

————— 'Afghan fight ends in death of 20 rebels', *New York Times*, 20 June 2005.

————— 'Taliban rebels still menacing Afghan south', *New York Times*, 2 March 2006.

Garrett, Stephen A., 'Terror Bombing of German Cities in World War II', in *Terrorism: The Philosophical Issues*, ed. Igor Primoratz (London: Palgrave Macmillan, 2004).

Geifman, A., *Thou Shalt Kill: Revolutionary Terrorism in Russia, 1894–1917* (Princeton, NJ: Princeton University Press, 1993).

Gettleman, Jeffrey, 'War in Sudan? Not where the oil wealth flows', *New York Times*, 24 October 2006.

Goldberg, Jeffrey, 'The unbranding: can Democrats make themselves look tough', *The New Yorker*, 21 March 2005.

Gordon, Michael R. and Trainor, Bernard E., 'Dash to Baghdad left top US generals divided', *New York Times*, 13 March 2006.

Gregoriadis, Solonis, *A History of Dictatorship* (Athens: Kapopoulos, 1975).

Hamas, 'Charter (August 1988)', in *Anti-American Terrorism and the Middle East*, ed. Barry Rubin and Judith Colp Rubin (Oxford and New York: Oxford University Press, 2002).

Hamburger, Peter, 'Song of the Holy War', *Quarterly Journal of Military History*, 18.4 (summer 2006).

Hare, R.M., *Moral Thinking: Its Levels, Method and Point* (Oxford: Clarendon Press, 1981).

Hezbollah, 'Program (February 1985)', in *Anti-American Terrorism and the Middle East*, ed. Barry Rubin and Judith Colp Rubin (Oxford and New York: Oxford University Press, 2002).

Kamp, Nina, O'Hanlon, Michael and Unikewicz, Amy 'The state of Iraq: an update,' *New York Times*, 16 June 2006.

Karampelas, Georgios, *Greek City Partisans, 1974–1985* (Athens: Grafes, 2002).

Keegan, John, *The Iraq War* (New York: Vintage Books/Random House, 2004, 2005).

————— *The First World War* (New York: Alfred A. Knopf, 1999).

Khosrokhavar, Farhad, *Suicide Bombers: Allah's New Martyrs* (London and Ann Arbor, MI: Pluto Press, 2005).

Kocieniewski, David, 'Rows of loosely guarded targets lie just outside New York City', *New York Times*, 9 May 2005.

Krasnov, V.N., 'Approaches to the Study of Suicide Terrorism', in *Pyschological Responses to the New Terrorism – A NATO – Russian Dialogue*, ed. S. Wessely (Amsterdam: IOS Press, 2005).

Kristof, Nicholas D. 'Genocide slow motion', *New York Review of Books*, 9 (February 2006).

————— 'Aid workers with guns', *New York Times*, 4 March 2007.

Laquer, Walter, *The New Terrorism: Fanaticism and the Arms of Mass Destruction* (Oxford and New York: Oxford University Press, 1999).

Lelyveld, Joseph, 'Jimmy Carter and apartheid', *New York Review of Books*, 29 March 2007.

Liddell Hart, B.H., *History of the Second World War* (New York: Putnam's, 1970).

Malinin, V., *Istoriya Russkogo Utopicheskogo Sotsialisma Vtoraya polovina 19 – nachalo 20 vv* (Moscow: Nauka, 1991).

Merkl, Peter H., *The Making of a Stormtrooper* (Princeton, NJ: Princeton University Press, 1980).

Miller, T. Christian, *Blood Money: Wasted Billions, Lost Lives and Corporate Greed in Iraq* (New York: Little, Brown, 2006).

MIPT terrorism knowledge base, 'Free Aceh Movement (GAM)', http://www.tkb.org/GroupID=3600, 10 May 2006 (accessed 4 June 2006).

Mitchell, Thomas G., *Native vs. Settler: Ethnic Conflict in Israel/Palestine, Northern Ireland and South Africa* (Westport, CT: Greenwood, 2000).

New York Times, editorial, 'Chemical time bombs', 10 May 2005.

Olivier, Anne Marie and Steinberg, Paul, *The Road to Martyrs' Square: A Journey into the World of the Suicide Bomber* (Oxford and New York: Oxford University Press, 2005).

Papaxelas, Alexis and Telloglou, Tasos, *17th November Investigation* (Athens: Estia, 2003).

Pape, Robert A., *Dying to Win: The Strategic Logic of Suicide Terrorism* (New York: Random House, 2005).

Papang, Hamid, 'Massacre of Muslims in Aceh–Sumatra revives calls for independence', http://www.muslimedia.com/archives/sea99/aceh-kill.htm., 16–31 May 1999 (accessed 4 June 2006).

Primoratz, Igor, 'What is Terrorism?', in *Terrorism: The Philosophical Issues*, ed. Igor Primorarz (New York: Palgrave Macmillan, 2004).

Prunier, Gerard, *Darfur: The Ambiguous Genocide* (Ithaca, NY: Cornell University Press, 2005).

Richardson, Louise, *What Terrorists Want* (New York: Random House, 2006). ✓ have

Rodin, David, 'Terrorism without intention', *Ethics*, July 2004.

Santora, Marc, 'One year later, Goldon Mosque is still in ruins', *New York Times*, 22 February 2007.

Scott, Richard, 'Scourge of the seas', *Jane's Defence Weekly*, 1 May 2005.

17 November, *The Proclamations* (Athens: Cactos, 2002).

Sharma Rajeev, *Beyond the Tigers: Tracking Rajeer Ghandi's Assassination* (New Delhi: Kaveri Books, 1998).

Skates, John Ray, *The Invasion of Japan: Alternative to the Bomb* (Columbia, SC: University of South Carolina Press, 1994).

Smith, Sebastian, *Allah's Mountains: The Battle for Chechnya* (London: Tauris, 2001).

Specter, Michael, 'Kremlin, Inc.', *The New Yorker*, 29 January 2007: 50–63.

Stephen, Ninian, 'Toward a Definition of Terrorism', *Terrorism and Justice,* ed. Tony Coady and Michael O'Keefe (Melbourne: Melbourne University Press, 2002).

Strachan, Hugh, *The First World War* (London: Penguin, 2005).

Sun Tzu, *The Art of War*, ed. James Clavell (New York: Dell, 1983).

Tantawi, Sheikh Muhammad Sayyed, 'Suicide Operations are Legitimate Defense (8 April 1997)', in *Anti-American Terrorism and the Middle East*, ed. Barry Rubin and Judith Colp Rubin (Oxford and New York: Oxford University Press, 2002).

Taylor, A.J.P., *A History of the First World War* (New York: Berkley, 1966).

Tierney, John, 'Bombs bursting in air', *New York Times*, 10 May 2005.

Tishkov, Valery, *Chechnya: Life in a War-Torn Society* (Berkeley, CA: University of California Press, 2004).

Tubbs, D.B., *Lancaster Bomber* (New York: Ballantine Books, 1972).

Walzer, Michael, *Just and Unjust Wars: A Moral Argument with Historical Illustrations* (New York: Basic Books, 1977).

Wikipedia: The Free Encyclopedia, 'Aceh', http://en.wikipedia.org/wiki/Aceh, accessed 6 June 2006.

———— 'Assassins', http://www.skewme.com/assassin.html., accessed 14 November 2006.

———— 'Provisional Irish Republican Army', http://www.answers.com/toic/provional-irish-republican-army, accessed 24 October 2006.

———— 'Sri Lanka', http://en.wikipedia.org/wiki/Ethnic_conflict_in_Sri_Lanka, accessed 15 June 2006.

Williams, Lea E., *Southeast Asia: A History* (Oxford and New York: Oxford University Press, 1976).

World Islamic Front, 'Statement: Jihad against Jews and Crusaders (23 February 1998)', in *Anti-American Terrorism and the Middle East*, ed. Barry Rubin and Judith Colp Rubin (Oxford and New York: Oxford University Press, 2002).

Zeiden, David, 'The Islamist View of Life as a Perennial Battle', in *Anti-American Terrorism and the Middle East,* ed. Barry Rubin and Judith Colp Rubin (Oxford and New York: Oxford University Press, 2002).

Index